HOW TO STOP USING DRUGS

BY ARNICE ROGERS

INTRODUCTION

IT'S 3 'O CLOCK IN THE MORNING. I'M SPRUNG, AND THE DEVIL HAS ME TRAPPED. I HAVE COME TO MY WIT'S END IN MY DESPERATE SEARCH FOR DRUGS. YET, I'M PARKED IN THE MIDDLE OF NOWHERE, SITTING IN MY CAR, ON A LONG PITCH DARK ROAD, IN A HEAVILY WOODED AREA WITH NO STREET LIGHTS, NO RESIDENTS, AND COMPLETE DARKNESS. THERE WAS NO ONE ELSE PRESENT ON THIS DARK, SCARY, EERIE NIGHT. NOT ANOTHER SOUL! EXCEPT ME, GOD, AND THE DEVIL! THUS, IN THIS BARREN WILDERNESS, THIS DESOLATE PLACE, THIS FORRESTRY OF A GRAVEYARD THAT I DUG FOR MYSELF, THERE WAS NO SIGN OF LIFE EXCEPT FOR MY OWN.

GOD REVEALED UNTO ME THE FRONT COVER AND CONTENTS OF THIS BOOK YEARS BEFORE IT WAS EVER THOUGHT OF OR WRITTEN. IN RETROSPECT, ON THIS DARK COUNTRY ROAD, I LOOKED OUT THE WINDOW OF MY CAR AND I SAW FROM THE BACKGROUND OF THE MOON THE WISE OWL WHO HELD A SERPENT IN ITS CLAWS.

REGARDLESS OF HOW THE SERPENT TWITCHED, TWIRLED OR TURNED, THE WISE OWL WAS NOT DISTURBED BY ITS MOVEMENTS. THE OWL HAD A FIRM GRIP ON THE SNAKE. BUT AS CLEVER AS A SNAKE IN THE DARK, THE OWL WAS YET WISER. THE SLIMY, SLITHERY, CAPTURED CREATURE COULD ONLY BEND UPWARDS LIKE A BOW; WHILE STRUGGLING IN VAIN TO FREE ITSELF FROM THE MASTER'S GRIP OF THE OWL'S CLAWS, AND LOOKING TOWARDS THE WISE OWL AND THE MOON ABOVE, THE EVIL SERPENT KNEW HE HAD FINALLY MET HIS FATE!

THIS VISION THAT GOD GAVE ME, AND THIS BOOK HE HAS INSPIRED THROUGH THAT VISION, IS ANOINTED BY GOD TO BREAK THE YOKE OF AN ADDICTION TOO AN ADDICTION, REGARDLESS TO WHAT'S YOUR ADDICTION. FOR AS SURE AS THE EYES OF THE WISE OWL ON THE FRONT COVER OF THIS BOOK WILL FOLLOW YOU WHEREVER YOU STAND, SIT, OR GO. THIS BOOK WILL DELIVER YOU FROM YOUR ADDICTION EVEN WHILE YOU ARE USING DRUGS. IT'S ANOINTED BY GOD TO DELIVER YOU, TALK TO YOU, AND SHOW YOU WHAT TO DO. THUS, IT WILL KEEP YOU READING UNTIL YOU

FIND YOU! THE YOKE OF DEMONIC DRUGS HAVE BEEN BROKEN! THAT YOU MAY UNDERSTAND THE MYSTERY OF YOUR ADDICTION. THE LORD SAYS WHATSOEVER THOU MAKE MANIFESTED IS LIGHT (Ephesians 5: 13). THEREFORE, KNOWLEDGE OF YOUR ADDICTION WILL DELIVER YOU FROM THE DARKNESS OF YOUR ADDICTION TO THIS WONDERFUL LIGHT THAT BE IN YOU.

LIKE THE WISE OWL WHO HELD THE SERPENT IN ITS CLAWS, YOU'LL NO LONGER BE IN THE DARKNESS OF YOUR ADDICTION. YOU'LL SEE THE DEVIL'S WORKS IN ALL THE EVIL, WICKED, AND SEDUCTIVE POWERS OF THE DRUGS. FOR YOU'LL SEE YOU, AND THIS DAY HAS GOD DELIVERED UNTO YOU THE SERPENT IN YOUR HANDS. FOR IT'S UP TO YOU WHETHER OR NOT THE SNAKE SHALL LIVE OR DIE!

IF YOU OR YOUR LOVED ONE HAS BEEN TRAPPED BY THE DEMONS OF AN ADDICTION, I PRAY THE LORD'S DELIVERANCE AT THE READING OF THIS BOOK. FOR THIS IS MORE THAN JUST A BOOK. IT'S YOUR LIFE! FOR AN ADDICTION IS AS SIN, AND THE WAGES OF SIN IS DEATH. (Romans 6: 23)!

DO YOU WANT TO LIVE?

ACKNOWLEDGEMENTS

GIVING HONOR TO MY BEAUTIFUL AND UNDERSTANDING WIFE. MISSIONARY: BARBARA J. ROGERS, WHO AS A PRAY WARRIOR OF THE LORD HAS SUFFERED MY ADDICTION WITH THE PRAYS OF THE SAINTS. FOR SHE'LL BEAR WITNESS TO GOD'S DELIVERANCE!

BROTHERLY LOVE GOES UNTO ARTIST, MR. LARRY EUGENE NIXON FOR THE DRAWING OF MY VISION, WHOM THE LORD SENT TO CHURCH WHEREAS I'M DEACON, THAT HE MAY REVEAL HIMSELF UNTO ME THROUGH LARRY'S ARTISTIC WORK.

GIVING HONOR UNTO MS. ALEXIS VICTORIAN, WHOM THE LORD HAS USED TO EDIT THIS DIVINE VISION IN ITS ENTIRETY THAT IT MAY BE CLEAR. THE LORD SAID WRITE THE VISION AND MAKE IT PLAIN (Habakkuk 2:2) IN WHICH I, MYSELF, DO NOT TAKE CREDIT FOR THE WORKS THE LORD WROUGHT THROUGH ME.

AS A DEACON OF THE MOST HIGH, AND A SON OF THE ALMIGHTY GOD! I PRAY GOD'S BLESSING TO ALL WHO HAVE DIED IN THEIR ADDICTIONS, AS WELL AS TO THOSE WHO STILL SUFFERS THE UNKNOWN FATE OF THEIR OWNS.

THE LORD HAS SPOKEN ON ADDICTION, AND IT'S DEMONIC!

FOR THE LORD HAS SHARPENED MY PEN AS A READY WRITER AND I SHALL NOT BEAR THY SWORD IN VAIN!

THUS, SAITH THE LORD ABOUT ADDICTIONS. FOR YOUR ADDICTION DOESN'T HAVE TO BE A DRUG. BUT YET, AS A DRUG. FOR THE LORD SPEAK ON ADDICTIONS AS DEMONIC, AND YOU AS A SINNER. WHEN YOU READ THESE WORDS THEY'RE TALKING DIRECTLY TO YOU! YOU'RE YOU AREN'T YOU?

GIVING HONOR UNTO GOD FOR CHRIST JESUS AT THE WRITING OF THIS BOOK. THE LORD WROTE THROUGH ANOTHER YOU TO YOU. THUS, DO YOU KNOW YOU KNOW YOU?

DEACON ARNICE ROGERS

PARABLE OF EVE'S ADDICTION

THUS, CONSIDER THE DEAD. THEY SHOULD REMIND YOU OF YOU. TOGETHER, THE TWO OF THEM LIVED A MIDDLE CLASS LIFE, BUT THEIR RELATIONSHIP WAS FAR FROM BEING MODEST. THERE WAS NOTHING HUMBLE ABOUT IT. SHE WAS THE MAN'S BOSS, RULER, COMPANION, AND HIS LOVER. YET, HE WAS SUPPOSED TO BE HER OLD MAN.

THEY HAVE LIVED TOGETHER SIX YEARS, BUT THE MAN ONLY RULED THE HOUSE WHEN SHE GAVE HIM HER PERMISSION. IN THE MEANWHILE, HE WOULD COME HOME FROM WORK, GET DRUNK, LOSE THE ARGUMENT, AND GO TO SLEEP. THIS WAS HIS ROUTINE EVERY NIGHT, AND SHE KNEW JUST HOW FAR HE WOULD GO WITH HER IN THEIR ARGUMENTS. HE WAS WELL TRAINED AND KNEW WHAT HE WAS DOING, BUT SO DID SHE.

SHE KNEW EVERYTHING ABOUT THE MAN, AND THERE WAS NOTHING ABOUT HIM SHE DIDN'T KNOW. SHE KNEW WHAT HE WOULD SAY WHEN HE CAME HOME FROM WORK AND HIS LAST WORDS BEFORE HE WENT TO BED. SHE HAD HIM WRAPPED AROUND HER FINGER AND EVERYONE WHO KNEW OF THEIR RELATIONSHIP FELT SORRY FOR THIS POOR MAN. THEY THOUGHT HE WAS A FOOL FOR BEING WITH SUCH A CLEVER WOMAN LIKE HER, ESPECIALLY SINCE SHE TREATED HIM LIKE A DOG.

SHE GAVE HIM COMMANDS AND LIKE AN OBEDIENT DOG, HE FOLLOWED INSTRUCTIONS. YET, HE WAS NEVER RIGHT ABOUT ANYTHING AROUND HER. IF HE WAS RIGHT, HE WAS STILL WRONG FOR BEING RIGHT. HE SHOULD HAVE NEVER OPENED HIS MOUTH, AND VOICED HIS MANLY OPINION. FOR HE WAS IN NO POSITION WITH HER TO MAKE DEMANDS. SHE WAS THE BOSS, AND THAT WAS THAT (Proverbs 21: 9).

FOR SIX YEARS, THEY LIVED TOGETHER AND THE MAN NEVER QUESTIONED HER RULES. HE LEARNED YEARS AGO THAT SHE WAS ALWAYS RIGHT REGARDLESS AS TO WHAT. SO, HE NEVER

QUESTIONED HER GOING AND HE NEVER QUESTIONED HER COMING. THUS, IN HIS EYES SHE COULD DO NO WRONG BECAUSE HE FELT LUCKY TO HAVE A GOOD LOOKING WOMAN LIKE HER. UNFORTUNATELY, HE PAID DEARLY TO HARNESS HER BEAUTY AND SHE OVERCHARGED HIM FOR HER LOVE AND HER TIME. SHE WAS SUCH A CLEVER WOMAN, BUT BEING SCORNED BY THE FEW MEN OF HER PAST, SHE MADE THIS ONE EARN HIS STAY. YET, HE WAS SO PROUD TO BE WITH HER, PROUD TO BE SEEN WITH HER, AND PROUD SHE WAS BOSS OF THE HOUSE, EVEN THOUGH SHE WAS NOT HIS WIFE. SHE WAS THE MOMMA HE NEVER HAD AND THE WHORE HIS FAMILY THOUGHT HE DIDN'T NEED, BUT SHE WAS THE TYPE OF WOMAN HE HAD ALWAYS WANTED. WOE!

HOWEVER, AFTER SIX MORE YEARS OF THE SAME OLD ROUTINE, SHE BECAME BORED WITH HER PRESENT SITUATION. THE WALLS TO THE PRISON SHE BUILT AROUND HERSELF WERE CLOSING IN ON HER. FOR SOME UNKNOWN GODLY REASON SHE WANTED OUT OF HER FARCE OF A RELATIONSHIP TO THE MAN, BUT SHE WAS STUCK! THERE WAS NO WAY OUT, YET SHE MUST ESCAPE! SHE NEEDED TO EXHALE! AND SHE YEARNED TO BE FREE!

THUS, WITHOUT HAVING GOD IN HER LIFE, THE SPIRIT OF HER ILL GOTTEN ESTATE BECAME LIKE A THORN IN HER SIDE AND HAVING NO COMFORTER, SHE KNEW SHE WAS STUCK! GOD STUCK HER WITH TREACHERY AND WITH ALL OF HER MISCHIEVOUS DEEDS, AND THE THORNS OF BOREDOM STUCK HER AS SINS! SHE WAS STUCK WITH A MAN SHE DIDN'T LOVE, STUCK ON THE GIFTS OF THE MAN WHO SHE FELT KEPT HER IN A PRISON AGAINST HER WILL, AND STUCK ON THE REOCCURRING THOUGHTS OF HOW WASTEFUL HER LIFE HAD BEEN BY DESPERATELY ACQUIRING MATERIAL THINGS WHILE HER NATURAL BEAUTY WAS BEING HIDDEN UNDER THE SHADOWS OF A WORTHLESS MAN.

SHE BLAMED THE MAN FOR EVERY THING THAT WAS WRONG IN HER GOD FORSAKEN LIFE. SHE DREADED HIS TOUCH REGARDLESS OF WHAT HE GAVE HER. SHE WAS TIRED OF

PRETENDING TO BE SATISFIED WITH HER PRESENT SITUATION. WITHOUT GOD IN HER LIFE, THE MATERIAL THINGS SHE SO DESIRED MEANT NOTHING TO HER ANYMORE. SOMETHING WAS TELLING HER TO LEAVE THE MAN AND WALK AWAY FROM IT ALL, BUT SHE WAS STUCK! GOD GAVE HER SPACE TO REPENT FOR HER SINS, BUT IN LOOKING BACK (Genesis 19: 26), SHE WAS FOOLISH, FOR BOREDOM PRICKED HER LIKE A SHARP THORN! SHE DIDN'T WANT TO GO BACK HOME TO HER FAMILY BECAUSE SHE KNEW WHAT THEY HAD TO OFFER WASN'T GOOD ENOUGH FOR HER.

THE ONLY REASON SHE PUT UP WITH THE MAN FOR THIS LONG WAS FOR HER FAMILY'S SAKE, BUT NOW SHE WAS TIRED OF EVERYTHING AND EVERYBODY TRYING TO TELL HER WHAT TO DO. SHE WANTED OUT. SHE WAS LEAVING AND KNEW SHE MUST GO, BUT SHE WAS RUNNING FROM A SPIRIT SHE DIDN'T KNOW WAS GOD; SO SHE WAS STUCK! THE WRATH OF GOD WAS UPON HER AND SHE WAS SICK TO HER STOMACH EVERY TIME THE MAN AND HER WERE TOGETHER.

THUS, THE WASTED YEARS SPENT ON ACQUIRING MATERIAL THINGS, AND THE FADING OF HER NATURAL BEAUTY WAS WHAT SHE WAS THINKING WHEN SHE MET YOU. SHE WAS TIRED OF HER SAME OLD FRIENDS AND SHE HAD NO CHILDREN OF HER OWN EXCEPT FOR THE HARD WORKING MAN WHO SHE MADE INTO HER CHILD. BUT ABOVE ALL OF HER DISCONTENTMENTS, SHE KNEW NOT THE LORD!

THERE WAS NOTHING SACRED IN HER HOUSE; NOT EVEN A BIBLE COULD BE FOUND AMONG ALL HER TREASURES. SHE HAD SUCH LOVELY TREASURES, BUT NONE WERE OF GOD AND THE LAST THING SHE WANTED TO HEAR WAS SOMETHING ABOUT GOD. ACCORDING TO HER NEIGHBORS, THE CLEVER WOMAN WASN'T TOO FAR FROM BEING A DEVIL, FOR SHE WAS ABOUT AS ROTTEN AS THEY COME, AS OLD FOLKS WOULD SAY. BUT THERE WAS NOTHING GOOD ANYONE HAD TO SAY ABOUT HER. THUS, AMONGST THE PEOPLE, SHE WAS ARROGANT, MANIPULATIVE, AND SNOBBISH. BUT IN HER BOSSY HOUSE, SHE WAS LOUD!

*CLAMOROUS! STUBBORN! AND CONTENTIOUS (Proverbs 9:13)
(Proverbs 27:15) (Proverbs 19:13) (Proverbs 21:19)!*

*THE MAN'S EVERYDAY ROUTINE BECAME BORING AS SIN AND
LIKE A YOUNG LAD, HE GOT IN HER WAY. SO, SHE TOOK TO
HERSELF SOME NEW FRIENDS, BUT YOU CAME WITH DRUGS!
SHE BECAME ADDICTED TO YOUR DRUGS AND WITHIN A FEW
WEEKS, HER MIDDLE CLASS HOME BECAME LIKE A COTTAGE IN
A CUCUMBER GARDEN. THEY CAME IN ALL SIZES AND EACH
NIGHT, WHEN THE MAN WOULD COME HOME FROM WORK, HE
WAS MET BY A DIFFERENT STRANGER GOING IN OR ONE
COMING OUT. THE WOMAN HAD STARTED USING HARD DRUGS.
BUT, STILL BEING THE BOSS OF THE HOUSE, HER MALE
FRIENDS WERE ALLOWED TO COME IN WITH OR WITHOUT THE
MAN'S PERMISSION. HE HAD NO SAY SO IN THE HOME. HE
DIDN'T RUN ANYTHING, FOR HE ONLY PAID THE BILLS
(Proverb 6: 26). WOE! MY LORD, THE GULLIBLE MAN WAS
WEAK WHEN IT CAME TO YOU. ALTHOUGH HE DIDN'T KNOW
HER FRIENDS, AFTER AN HOUR OF STEADILY DRINKING FREE
LIQUOR, THEY BECAME GOOD COMPANY. DID YOU ENJOY
YOURSELF THOSE DEADLY NIGHTS? YOU USED TO LOVE GOING
TO HER HOUSE WHEN THE MAN WAS AT WORK OR NOT THERE.
HOW MANY TIMES HAVE YOU SEDUCED HER OFF OF YOUR
CRUMBS BEFORE SHE DEMANDED A BIGGER HIT?*

*THE LITTLE MAN WOULD COME HOME FROM WORK, GET
DRUNK, AND GO TO THE STORE FOR MORE ALCOHOL WHILE
THE WOMAN WALKED AROUND HALF NAKED, FIENDING FOR
MORE DRUGS. YET, IN HIS ABSENCE, SHE DID AS SHE PLEASED,
BUT ONCE HE RETURNED, SHE WAS ALWAYS MAD BECAUSE HE
GOT IN THE WAY OF HER GOOD HITS! THUS, SINCE THE DAY
HER ADDICTION BEGAN, SHE HAS NEVER HAD A BAD HIT. SHE
WAS AS GREEDY WHEN IT CAME TO DRUGS AS SHE WAS WITH
EVERYTHING ELSE. YOUR DRUGS WERE WHAT SHE NEEDED TO
BREAK HER EVERYDAY MONOTONY. THE UNIMAGINABLE HIGH
GAVE HER THE FEELING OF BEING FREE. AT LEAST, THAT'S
WHAT SHE THOUGHT, BUT SHE COULDN'T SEE THE TROUBLES
OF GOD THAT WERE ABOUT TO BEFALL HER. SHE COULDN'T*

SEE THE NEIGHBORS WHO NO LONGER LOOKED THE OTHER WAY, NOR COULD SHE HEAR THE MALICIOUS GOSSIP ON HER FAMILY'S LIPS. THE HIGH FREED HER FROM ALL CONCERNS, BUT WHAT SHE DIDN'T KNOW WAS FROM THAT DAY FORWARD, SHE WOULD EAT A THIRD OF HELL'S FIRE HITTING THE PIPE AND BLACK, BURNED BLISTERS WOULD SCORCH HER PRETTY LIPS WHILE TRYING TO HOLD ON TO THESE UNGODLY FEELINGS. WOE! FOR SHE JUST LOVED THE HIGH AND THE ATTENTION SHE GOT WHEN SHE WALKED INTO THE ROOM.

SHE WAGGED A MEAN TAIL AND SHE WAS A GOOD-LOOKING, PROVOCATIVE WOMAN WITH GREEN, PENETRATING EYES THAT SAW THE CORE OF A MAN'S LUST. SHE WAS JUST THE KIND OF WOMAN YOU NEEDED TO GET INTO TROUBLE, BUT YOU KNEW THIS BEFORE YOU TURNED HER OUT ON DRUGS. WOE! YOU COULDN'T WAIT TO SEDUCE HER WITH YOUR FREAKY LUST. HER TOUCH WAS ENOUGH TO KEEP YOU ON THE PIPE AND KNOCKING AT THE MAN'S DOOR WITH DRUGS EACH AND EVERY OTHER NIGHT UNTIL YOU FOUND OUT THAT OTHERS CAME WITH HER ADDICTION. WOE! FOR HER NAME IS "EVE" (Genesis 3:20) AND SHE HAD KNOWLEDGE OF YOU "ADAM," BEFORE THE FALL (Genesis 3). WOE! SHE HAD THE SENSE TO COACH THIS GOD-FORSAKEN MAN TO BUILD HER A DREAM HOUSE, BUT BECAUSE OF YOU, HER DRUG ADDICTION, AND UNGODLY WAYS IT WILL SOON BE DESTROYED WITHIN A MATTER OF MONTHS. MY GOD! YET, SHE DIDN'T KNOW THIS, BUT SHE WAS ABOUT TO LEARN SOON ENOUGH AS SHE CONTINUED TO HIDE HER ADDICTION FROM HER SO CALLED MAN. THUS, THE MAN WITH WHOM SHE WOULDN'T CONSIDER AS HER MAN, NOR SOMEONE WHO SHE COULD EVEN RESPECT. THE POOR MAN WAS BROUGHT TO SHAME MANY TIMES BEFORE FAMILY AND FRIENDS, BUT HE NEVER FELT RIDICULED BY HER INSULTS.

SHE WAS ALWAYS UP FRONT WITH THE MAN. SHE MADE IT CLEAR TO HIM FROM THE START THAT SHE DIDN'T LOVE HIM. SHE TOLD HIM SHE WAS WAITING ON THE RIGHT MAN, BUT THAT WAS 18 YEARS AGO. SHE EXPLAINED TO THE MAN WHAT

SHE NEEDED WAS AN OX TO CARRY HER LOAD AND BECAUSE OF HER BEAUTY, HE AGREED WHOLE-HEARTEDLY TO THEIR ARRANGEMENT. SHE NEARLY LAUGHED WHEN SHE THOUGHT OF THEIR RELATIONSHIP AS "BEAUTY AND THE BEAST" EVEN THOUGH HE HAD THE STRENGTH OF AN OX AND GAVE HER EVERYTHING SHE NEEDED AND NEARLY ALL OF WHATEVER THE CLEVER HEIFER WANTED. SHE LIVED BETTER THAN THE REST OF HER FAMILY AND HER HOUSE WAS MUCH BIGGER THAN ALL HER NEIGHBORS. SO, NOT ONLY DID SHE OWN THE LOVELY HOUSE, BUT SHE WAS BOSS OF IT! SHE DROVE ANOTHER CAR ANYTIME SHE PREFERRED A NEW ONE AND SHE WORE SOME OF THE BEST DESIGNER CLOTHES ON THE MARKET. THUS, BEING UPPER MIDDLE CLASS, SHE WAS A HIGH-MINDED WOMAN. YOU COULDN'T TELL HER ANYTHING, YOU HAD TO ASK HER SOMETHING, AND WHEN YOU ASK HER SOMETHING SHE WOULD ANSWER WHEN SHE'S MOVING OR ON THE RUN. SHE DIDN'T HAVE TIME FOR ANYTHING THAT DIDN'T MAKE CENTS. HER MOTTO WAS SIMPLE: IF IT DIDN'T MAKE DOLLARS, IT WASN'T WORTH HER TIME. SHE WAS SUCH A CLEVER WOMAN AND WITH THE STRENGTH OF HER OX, SHE ACCUMULATED MUCH. BUT ALL OF WHAT SHE HAD ACCUMULATED, SHE HELD UNDER ONE RULE: HERS! THUS, UNTIL HER DRUG ADDICTION GOT OUT OF CONTROL. WOE!

DURING THE FIRST TRIMESTER OF HER PROGRESSIVE DRUG ADDICTION, IT GOT TO WHERE SHE COULD NO LONGER HIDE IT FROM THE MAN. HE STARTED SNOOPING AROUND LIKE AN OLD DOG AND SHE SENSED HE SMELLED SOMETHING WAS WRONG. TOO MUCH MONEY WAS BEING SPENT, BILLS WERE BEING RETURNED UNPAID, AND SHE PUT LAST MONTH'S HOUSE PAYMENT ON THE PIPE. WOE! FRANTICALLY, NOT KNOWING WHAT TO DO, NOT KNOWING WHERE TO TURN, AND NOT KNOWING HOW TO EXPLAIN HER ADDICTION TO THE MAN. GOOD GOD ALMIGHTY! SHE INTRODUCED THE MAN TO DRUGS, AND WOE! WHAT A MISTAKE! THE MILD-TEMPERED MAN BECAME A BEAST OVERNIGHT AND UNLIKE BEFORE WHEN HE WAS DUMB, NAIVE, AND GULLIBLE, WHEN HE HIT THE PIPE, HIS EYES BUCKED AND HIS MOUTH FLEW WIDE OPEN! THUS,

HE BECAME THE MONSTER SHE THOUGHT HE HAS ALWAYS LOOKED LIKE. HE WAS OBSESSED WITH THE DRUGS AND FELL IN LOVE WITH THE PIPE. HE NO LONGER WORKED EXCEPT ON FEEDING HIS ADDICTION AND HIS OBSESSION TO DRUGS KEPT HER WORKING DAY AND NIGHT TO SUPPLY THEIR HABIT. NOW, HE FOLLOWS HER WHEREVER SHE GOES AND IF SHE SNUCK OFF WITHOUT HIM, HE WOULD LAY HANDS ON HER IF SHE RETURNED WITHOUT DRUGS. FOR THE DRUGS TRANSFORMED THE LITTLE DANGEROUS MAN FROM MEASLY PREY TO A PREDATOR, OVERNIGHT.

WHEN HE BIT INTO THE APPLE (hit the pipe), HE SAW HIS CALLING. THE DRUGS DECEIVED THE MAN BECAUSE HE DIDN'T SEE HIMSELF AS A MERE MAN OR AS A HEN PECKED WEAKLING. HE SAW SOMETHING WITHIN HIMSELF MUCH MORE SINISTER, EVIL, AND WICKED. THUS, BEING SEDUCED BY DRUGS AND OVERLOOKING THE LORD, THE MAN SAW HIMSELF AS A DEVIL. WOE! THE DEMON IN HIS EYES SCARED HER, FOR SHE TOO SAW THE SAME THING AND KNEW FROM THAT DAY FORTH SHE WOULD BECOME HIS SEX SLAVE UNTO HER DEATH. MY LORD, FOR SHE BECAME THE ONLY THING SWEET ABOUT HIM IN HIS HOUSE AND ALL HER FRIENDS WHO HAD DRUGS JUST LOVED HER WHENEVER THEY GOT A CHANCE. THE DOOR WAS CRACKED TO ANYONE WHO HAD DRUGS, NEEDED TO USE A PIPE, OR WAS WILLING TO SHARE A DECENT HIT! THE HOUSE WAS DARK YET, THEY HAD NO IDEA. MY GOD, THEY JUST DIDN'T KNOW AND EVEN UNTIL THIS DAY. THEY STILL DON'T KNOW THAT YOU WERE THERE. YOU! WHAT? THE DEVIL KNEW IT WAS YOU AND HE'S HOPING FOR YOUR RETURN. YOU HELPED HIM A LOT AND YOU KNEW THIS WHEN YOU TOOK DRUGS TO THE MAN'S HOUSE. YOU KNEW THIS BEFORE YOU SEDUCED THE MAN'S WOMAN, SISTERS, AND THEIR DAUGHTERS.

YET, THE TWO OF THEM WERE GOOD FOR ONE ANOTHER, BUT IN A BAD WAY. HE NEEDED HER TO BECOME THE DEVIL HE BECAME AND SHE NEEDED HIM TO BECOME A WHORE WITHOUT SHAME. WOE! SHE LOST EVERYTHING BEHIND THAT HIT AND SHE NOW CLINGS TO LIFE ON THE BROKEN NAILS OF

HER DEMONIC ADDICTION. THE HOUSE SHE ONCE RULED OVER AS HERS, HAS BEEN PUT ON THE PIPE AND THUS, HAS GONE UP IN SMOKE. THE CARS SHE USED TO DRIVE AT WILL, HAVE BEEN PUT ON THE PIPE AND THUS, GONE UP IN SMOKE. THE BUSINESS THE MAN ONCE MANAGED AND OWNED, HAS BEEN PUT ON THE PIPE AND THUS, GONE UP IN SMOKE. YET, ALL THAT REMAINS ARE THEIR ADDICTIONS AND THE LOSS OF HER NATURAL BEAUTY. WOE! TODAY, IN HER HIGH-MINDEDNESS, THE FAMILY POINTS THEIR FINGERS AT HER AND THE NEIGHBORS HAVE BEGUN TO WHISPER. MY LORD!

THE GORILLA ON HIS BACK KEPT HER WORKING DAY AND NIGHT TO SUPPLY THEIR HABIT. HE'S NOT NICE TO HER ANY MORE. HIS GORILLA NEEDS DRUGS AT ALL TIMES AND HE'S CONSIDERED ONE OF THE MOST DANGEROUS DRUG ADDICTS ON THE STREETS. HOWEVER, BEFORE THAT BIG HIT, SHE HAD STRIPPED HIM OF ALL HIS POWER, SHAMED HIM BEFORE FAMILY AND FRIENDS, AND ROBBED HIM OF ALL HIS PRIDE. HE WAS A FOOL, A MOMMA'S BOY, AND CRY BABY OF A MAN. THIS, SHE KNEW BEFORE THAT BIG HIT, FOR SHE WAS USED TO HIM BEING LIKE A LITTLE PUPPY, A GOOD DOG, AND FOLLOWING ALL HER ORDERS. BUT, SINCE THAT DEMONIC HIT, EVERYTHING CHANGED. IRONICALLY, BEFORE THE HIT, SHE WAS BOSS! BUT NOW, HE TELLS HER WHAT TO DO, WHERE TO DO IT, HOW TO DO IT, AND WHEN TO DO IT. THUS, IF SHE DOESN'T DO IT RIGHT, SHE'LL HAVE PROBLEMS. THE LITTLE MAN WHO SHE THOUGHT LOOKED SO MUCH LIKE A MONSTER BECAME A REAL MONSTER ON DRUGS. HE HAD NO FEAR IN HIS ADDICTION AND BECAME JUST AS CLEVER AS HER. WHENEVER HER FRIENDS WOULD VISIT, HE STILL DIDN'T MIND AS LONG AS HE WAS ABLE TO HIDE IN THE CLOSET AND STEAL THEIR MONEY AND DRUGS, LEAVING HER TO BLAME. HE PLAYED THE WAIT GAME LIKE A SPIDER AND HELPED HER EAT ALL THE FLIES THEY CAUGHT IN HER WEB.

UNFORTUNATELY, BEFORE THE MAN'S DEATH, HE HAD A CHANCE TO KNOW GOD, BUT IN HIS ADDICTION, HE CHOSE TO BE A DEVIL. BEFORE HIS ADDICTION, HE HAD A CHANCE TO BE A MAN, BUT HE WAS RULED BY A WOMAN. HE HAD A CHANCE

TO BE SAVED, BUT LIKE A FOOL, HE DIDN'T WANT TO BE SAVED (Luke 12: 20). HE FELL IN LOVE WITH THE EVIL THAT CAME WITH DRUGS BECAUSE IT BROUGHT OUT HIS TRUE SELF. FOR "YOU ARE WHICHEVER YOU ARE." HE STARTED TAKING MONEY FROM OTHER ADDICTS AND ROBBING DOPE DEALERS FOR DRUGS TO SUPPORT THEIR HABBITS. SHE BURNT HERSELF OUT WALKING DAY AND NIGHT, GOING UP AND DOWN THE STREETS. WOE! HOWEVER, NO BAD DEED GOES UNPUNISHED. IN THE DOPE GAME, THE STREETS TALK AND AFTER THE MAN'S LAST HIT, HE FELL INTO A DEEP SLEEP.

AS FOR THE WOMAN, TODAY SHE'S QUIET AND KEEPS TO HERSELF, FOR SHE HAS NO FRIENDS. GREAT WAS THE FALL OF HER HOUSE! HER FRIENDS LEFT WITH PIPES IN THEIR HANDS LOOKING FOR ANOTHER PLACE TO RUIN. MY LORD! YOU'LL NOT SEE HER DURING THE HOUR OF A DAY. SHE HIDES HER ADDICTION IN THE DARK OF THE NIGHT. SHE'S FRAGILE, TIMID, AND VERY CAREFUL NOT TO DRAW ATTENTION TO HERSELF. SHE DOESN'T WANT TO BE SEEN. THE BEAUTIFUL BODY HAS BEEN BADLY ABUSED AND WORN OUT BY THE MEN OF HER ADDICTION. WOE! THE MEAN TAIL THAT CAUSED SO MUCH DAMAGE NO LONGER WAGS. THE LOVELY CITY OF BABYLON HAS DIMINISHED (Revelation 17: 5) (Isaiah 47: 5)! THUS, IT VANISHED INTO A PUFF OF THIN AIR. THE WRATH OF GOD WAS GREAT UPON HER WHOREDOM! AND SHE KNOWS NOT UNTIL THIS DAY FORTH "LEST THOU SHOULDEST PONDER THE PATH OF LIFE, HER WAYS ARE MOVEABLE, THAT THOU CANST NOT KNOW THEM" (Proverbs 5: 6). THUS, SAITH THE LORD!

THE NEIGHBORS ARE HAPPY SHE'S GONE AND IT SATISFIED HER FAMILY'S BELIEF THAT SHE HAD FINALLY MET HER FATE. "SHE HAD IT COMING TO HER ALL THE TIME" THEY WOULD SAY TO THEMSELVES. THEY WERE SICK AND TIRED OF HER ALWAYS BEGGING FOR MONEY TO BUY DRUGS. NOW SHE KNOWS FIRST HAND WHAT IT IS TO BE WITHOUT. "MISS HIGH AND MIGHTY GETS NO MERCY FROM ME" SAYS HER FAMILY. YET, THEIR HOMES ARE FILLED WITH ALL HER PRECIOUS SUBSTANCES THAT THEY BOUGHT THROUGH HER ADDICTION, FOR PENNIES ON THE

DOLLAR. WOE! "NO SIR, MISS HIGH AND MIGHTY GETS NO MERCY FROM ME! I REMEMBER WHEN SHE DID THIS AND I REMEMBER WHEN SHE DID THAT." THIS IS WHAT HER FAMILY SAYS WHILE ENJOYING THE LUXURY OF HER COMFORTS. MY GOD!

WITH THE LOSS OF THE MEAN TAIL SHE WAGGED SO WELL AND THE UNATTRACTIVENESS OF HER NATURAL BEAUTY, SHE NO LONGER CAN TURN FAVORS FOR DRUGS. FOR SHE DEPENDS SOLELY ON HER MOUTH TO SUPPLY HER HABIT. BUT YOU SAY SHE'S MUCH BETTER IF SHE DOESN'T SPEAK. YET, WHEN SHE OPENS WIDE HER MOUTH, SHE SPITS OUT THE MORBID SOUL OF YOU!

A CERTAIN MAN

THERE WAS A CERTAIN MAN WHO WAS ADDICTED TO THE "METHODOLOGY," AND "PROCESS" OF HOW HE USED DRUGS. HE THOUGHT HE WAS ADDICTED TO DRUGS, FOR THE DRUGS CONFUSED THE MAN AND IN HIS ADDICTION HE DIDN'T KNOW WHETHER HE WAS ADDICTED TO DRUGS OR THE PIPE. ALL HE KNEW WAS THAT HE ENJOYED DRUGS AND LOVED THE NAKED PLEASURES THAT CAME WITH HIS DRUG USAGE.

HOWEVER, AFTER USING THE DRUG FOR THREE YEARS, THE DRUGS TURNED ON THE MAN. INSTEAD OF HIM ENJOYING DRUGS, THE DRUGS NOW SCARED HIM. HIS LONG USAGE OF DRUGS ADDICTED HIM AND THE DEVIL TORMENTED HIM DAY AND NIGHT WITH UNKNOWN FEARS. THE MAN NO LONGER WANTED TO USE DRUGS, BUT DESPITE THE FACT THAT HE NO LONGER WANTED TO USE DRUGS, HE STILL USED DRUGS. THEREFORE, HE UNDERSTOOD THAT IT MUST BE SOMETHING WITHIN HIMSELF THAT KEPT HIM ADDICTED TO DRUGS. THUS, THE DRUGS HE SO LEARNED TO HATE. FOR IT WAS HIS DESIRE TO NOT USE DRUGS, BUT HIS DESIRE WAS ONLY A DESIRE. HIS SPIRIT WAS WILLING, BUT HIS FLESH WAS WEAK (Matthew 26: 41). AND AS SURE AS ANOTHER DAY WOULD COME AND GO, THE MAN USED DRUGS.

SO, HE BEGAN TO STUDY HIS ADDICTION AND GAVE INTO THE FEELING HE FELT WHEN HE USED DRUGS. HE SAW IT WAS THE SAME FEELING ADAM AND EVE FELT WHEN THEY BIT INTO THE FORBIDDEN FRUIT (Genesis 2: 16-17). THEY BOTH KNEW SIN AND SAW THEIR NAKEDNESS. THUS, AFTER THE MAN'S FIRST HIT ON THE PIPE HE TOO SAW THE SAME THING AND FELT NAKED. BUT, SINCE HE WAS HELPLESS TO THE DEMONIC FORCE THAT GAVE HIM DRIVE, HE ALLOWED THE PIPE TO DRIVE HIM EVERY PLACE HE DIDN'T WANT TO GO. ALL HE COULD DO WAS FREAK OFF THE HIGH WHILE SHE HELD HIS HEAD IN HER LAP. THE MAN HATED EVERYTHING HE WAS DOING, BUT HE COULDN'T HELP FROM BEING A VICTIM OF HIS DEMONIC ADDICTION. HE COULD'NT HELP FROM LOOKING ON THE FLOOR FOR DRUGS HE NEVER DROPPED, PEEPING OUT WINDOWS THINKING SOMEONE WAS COMING, AND BECOMING EXTREMELY SCARED EVERY TIME HE HIT THAT GOD FORSAKEN PIPE. THERE WAS NOTHING HE COULD DO ABOUT HIS ADDICTION EXCEPT SUFFER THE WAIT ON HIS NEXT HITS. HE FOUND HIMSELF LIKE A MAN LOOKING FOR WATER IN DRY PLACES (Psalm 105: 41) (Isaiah 58: 11) AND TURNING OVER EVERY ROCK IN TOWN TRYING TO FIND SOME.

HE KNEW THE WELL TO HIS ADDICTION RAN AS DEEP AS THE GROUND WORE HARD ON THE MAN'S FEET IN HIS DAILY SEARCH FOR DRUGS. HE KNEW HE MUST BREAK THE YOKE OF THE DEVIL (Isaiah 10: 27). THE DRUGS WERE TAKING HIM TOO FAST. EVERY TIME HE GOT HIGH, THE DEVIL APPEARED. HE LOVED TO SMOKE WITH ONLY WOMEN, THUS HE DIDN'T KNOW WHICH ONE WAS WORSE, THE WOMEN OR THE DRUGS! ALL HE KNEW WAS THAT HE WOULD LEAVE HOME WITH A POCKET FULL OF MONEY AND COME BACK BROKE, SCARED, AND SMELLING LIKE A WHOREHOUSE. WOE! THE MAN KNEW HE WAS DYING FROM DRUGS AND GOD REVEALED UNTO HIM THAT HE WAS ONE HIT AWAY FROM DEATH! YET, HE KNEW IT WAS IMPOSSIBLE FOR HIM TO STOP USING DRUGS JUST AS HE KNEW IT WAS IMPOSSIBLE FOR HIM NOT TO TAKE ANOTHER HIT. HE REMEMBERED ONE THING HIS MOTHER HAD ALWAYS PREACHED TO HIM AS A CHILD AND THAT WAS THAT ALL

THINGS ARE POSSIBLE WITH GOD (Matthew 19: 26).

THEREFORE, THE MAN SINCERELY PRAYED OVER HIS DRUGS BEFORE HE USED THEM AND ASKED GOD TO TAKE THE STING OF DEATH OUT OF EACH HIT. EVERY TIME HE USED DRUGS, HE PRAYED AND THE DEMONS INSIDE THE MAN WOULD PUKE AT THE MENTIONING OF THE LORD'S PRAYER (Matthew 6: 9-13). "LORD, YOU SAY PUT GOD FIRST IN ALL THINGS (Matthew 6: 33), SO I ASK THAT YOU BLESS THIS PIECE OF DOPE BEFORE I USE IT THAT IT MAY CAUSE ME NO HARM." THE DEVIL BEING IN THE USERS AROUND HIM MADE THEM THINK HE WAS CRAZY. THE MAN WOULD QUOTE A SCRIPTURE BEFORE HE USED DRUGS AND THE PIPE WOULD NAIL HIM TO THE CROSS. MY GOD! HE WOULD ROLL ON THE GROUND, FOAM AT THE MOUTH, JUMP UP, AND TAKE OFF RUNNING DOWN THE STREET HALF NAKED. WOE! THE DEMONIC DRUGS WOULD TOTALLY POSSESS HIS MIND AND THE DEVIL WORKED HIM LIKE A PUPPET. SATAN HAD THE MAN DOING THINGS THAT ONLY A DEVIL WOULD HAVE YOU TO DO AND THERE WAS NOTHING GODLY ABOUT IT. THUS, DESPICABLE THINGS NOT NEEDED MENTIONING OF AND AN ABOMINATION WORTHY OF DEATH. WOE!

HOWEVER, DESPITE ALL OF THE SINFUL THINGS THE DRUGS HAD THE MAN DOING, YET GOD WAS WITH THE MAN AND IN HIS DAILY SUFFERING HE WAS LEARNING FROM HIS ADDICTION. "BLESSED IS THE MAN TO WHOM THE LORD WILL NOT IMPUTE SIN" (Romans 4: 8).

IN HIS STUDY, HE LEARNED THAT HIS DRUG ADDICTION WAS A DEMONIC ADDICTION OF SPIRITUAL WARFARE TAKING PLACE WITHIN THE SUBCONSCIOUS MIND. HE LEARNED WHEN YOU USE DRUGS, YOU ENTER THE SPIRITUAL WORLD OF YOUR SUBCONSCIOUS MIND AND THE DEVIL COME UPON YOU WITH SUDDEN FEAR. HOWEVER,

DURING THOSE FRIGHTENING MOMENTS OF YOUR HIGH, SATAN IS TRYING TO LOCK YOU INTO THAT SCARY STATE OF YOUR SUBCONSCIOUS MIND SO ALL YOU'LL SEE IS DEATH. WOE! PLEASE HELP US LORD!

IN THE SPIRIT, HE SAW THE SUBCONSCIOUS MIND AS A GRAVEYARD FOR THE DEVIL AND EVERY TIME YOU GET HIGH, THE DEAD ARE AMONG YOU. YOU HAVE CROSSED THE OZONE LAYER BEYOND THE CONSCIOUS STATE OF YOUR CARNAL MIND AND YOU WERE FORBIDDEN BY GOD TO NOT ENTER THE DOMAIN OF YOUR SUBCONSCIOUS MIND. GOD SAID "PRAY AND BE WATCHFUL" (Luke 21: 36), BUT WHILE IN YOUR SUBCONSCIOUS MIND, YOU'RE IN THE WORKSHOP OF THE DEVIL WITHOUT A CONSCIOUS THOUGHT. MY LORD!

HE LEARNED THAT WHEN SATAN LOCKED YOU INTO YOUR SUBCONSCIOUS STATE OF MIND, YOU WERE BEING SURROUNDED BY THE DEAD. YOU WILL DIE TRYING TO RUN FROM DEATH, TO DEATH. MY GOD! PLEASE HELP US LORD! IN THE WORKSHOP OF THE DEVIL, THERE'S NO WAY OUT AND YOU WILL NOT ESCAPE FROM THAT DRUG-INDUCED, FRIGHTFUL MOMENT OF WHATEVER BAD EXPERIENCE YOU'RE GOING THROUGH WHICH WILL EVENTUALLY LEAD TO YOUR DEMISE. MY GOD!

SATAN HAS BLOCKED ALL EXITS BACK INTO YOUR CONSCIOUS STATE OF MIND, AND GOOD GOD ALMIGHTY! YOU HAVE SEEN HIS FACE! WOE! HE SAW THE DEVIL'S WORKS IN ALL THE EVIL, WICKED, SEDUCTIVE, AND DEMONIC POWERS OF THE DRUGS. THE WEAKENING OF THE CARNAL MIND AND THOSE CAUGHT IN THE WEBS OF THEIR DEMONIC ADDICTIONS HANG FROM ALL POINTS OF DEATH. THEY ARE WILLING TO DO ANYTHING AT ANY TIME AND AT ANY PLACE FOR DRUGS. PLEASE HELP US LORD! HE LEARNED THAT HIS DESIRE TO GET OFF DRUGS WAS LESSER THAN HIS DESIRE TO ACQUIRE DRUGS. ONLY THROUGH HIS TRYING EFFORTS DID GOD DELIVER HIM FROM THE METHODOLOGY AND PROCESS OF HOW TO USE DRUGS. HALLELUJAH! FOR GOD REVEALED TO THE MAN THE MYSTERY OF AN ADDICTION AND HOW TO STOP USING DRUGS. THANK YOU JESUS OF NAZARETH!

THE SPIRITUAL WORLD OF YOUR SUBCONSCIOUS MIND

ILLICIT DRUGS (street drugs), SUCH AS HEROIN, METH, CRACK, PCP, ACID AND OTHER MAN-MADE HALLUCINATORY DRUGS ARE THUS FAR, THE GREATEST WEAPON SATAN HAS USED AGAINST GOD, SOCIETY, AND YOU. THE DEVIL KNOWS WHEN YOU USE MIND ALTERING DRUGS, YOU ENTER INTO A THREE DIMENSIONAL STATE OF MIND, BETTER KNOWN AS THE SPIRTUAL WORLD. THE SPIRITUAL WORLD EXISTS IN YOUR SUBCONSCIOUS MIND, BUT THE DEVIL ALSO LIVES IN YOUR SUBSCONSIOUS MIND. THUS, ARE YOU NOT AWARE THAT THE SUBCONSCIOUS MIND IS THE WORKSHOP OF THE DEVIL? YOU ARE NOT CONSCIOUS OF YOUR SUBCONSCIOUS MIND, WHILE YOU'RE SUBCONSCIOUSLY CONSCIOUS THAT YOU'RE IN THE SPIRITUAL WORLD, ALSO KNOWN AS BEING "HIGH". THERE IS NOTHING CONCEPTUAL, PHYSICAL, OR PERCEPTUAL ABOUT IT. YOU'RE IN A THREE DIMENSIONAL TRANSITIONAL STATE OF MIND WHERE YOU'RE BEING TORMENTED WITH FEAR, BEING VEXED BY DEMONIC SPIRITS, AND BEING POSESSED BY THE DEVIL. WOE! WHEN YOU ENTER INTO THE SPIRITUAL WORLD OF YOUR SUBCONSCIOUS MIND OR WHEN YOU GET "HIGH" YOU UNKNOWINGLY WITNESS THE WAR WITHIN YOU BETWEEN GOOD AND EVIL, FOR "YOU ARE WHICHEVER YOU ARE."

THE WAR WITHIN

THE BIBLE SAYS YOU WRESTLE NOT AGAINST FLESH AND BLOOD, BUT AGAINST PRINCIPALITIES, AGAINST POWERS, AGAINST THE RULERS OF THE DARKNESS OF THIS WORLD, AND AGAINST SPIRITUAL WICKEDNESS IN HIGH PLACES (Ephesians 6: 12). IN OTHER WORDS, YOU DON'T WAGE WAR AGAINST SISTER, BROTHER, OR FRIENDS. THE WAR WITHIN YOU IS AGAINST THE DEVIL. NOTICE, WHEN YOU ADD THE NUMBERS SIX AND TWEVE, IT EQUALS 18. THE MARK OF THE BEAST IS

*666. YOU MAY NOT UNDERSTAND THAT 666 EQUALS "18"
WHICH IS THE MARK OF THE DEVIL (Revelations 13: 17-18).
ACCORDING TO THIS SCRIPTURE, THE WAR WITHIN YOU IS
BETWEEN YOU, GOD, AND THE DEVIL. THEREFORE, LET US
PRAY THAT GOD IS WITH YOU WHEN YOU ENTER INTO THE
SPIRITUAL WORLD OF YOUR SUBCONSCIOUS MIND. YOU WILL
THINK IT'S ANOTHER PERSON, PLACE, OR THING THAT WILL
GET YOU, BUT ALL THE WHILE IT'S THE DEVIL. YOUR
ADDICTION TO DRUGS ARE BEYOND NOTHING THAT YOU
ALREADY KNOW, FOR YOU KNOW IT'S THE DEVIL THAT KEEPS
YOU ADDICTED TO DRUGS.*

LIVING IN FEAR

*UNDERSTAND YOU! THE REASON YOU GET HIGH IS BECAUSE YOU
LIKE LIVING IN FEAR. YET, THE FEAR THAT COMES FROM YOUR
GETTING HIGH IS NOTHING COMPARED TO THE SUFFERING THAT
COMES FROM YOUR DEMONIC ADDICTION. YOUR ADDICTION TO
FEAR KEEPS YOU ADDICTED TO DRUGS AND YOUR SPIRIT, WHILE
IN TRANSITION, IS FIGHTING AGAINST SATAN'S ARMY TO HELP
YOU GET BACK INTO YOUR CONSCIOUS STATE OF MIND. THE
HALLUCINOGENIC THINGS YOU THOUGHT YOU SAW, THE
UNEXPLAINED EVENTS, AND THE OUT-OF-BODY EXPERIENCES
WERE SUBCONSCIOUSLY REAL, BUT MENTALLY, YOU WERE JUST
HIGH. YET, SOMEHOW IN YOUR DRUG-INDUCED STATE, YOU
WERE AWARE OF SATAN'S LITTLE IMPS ENCAMPED AROUND YOU,
WAITING FOR YOU TO CROAK SO THAT THEY COULD DRAG YOUR
FRIGHTENED LITTLE SOUL TO HELL!*

KNOW THE GOD IN YOU

*LEARNING HOW TO STOP USING DRUGS IS AS SIMPLE AS
KNOWING GOD IS IN YOU. THUS, DO YOU KNOW GOD IS IN YOU?
IF NOT, HOW CAN YOU STOP USING DRUGS NOT KNOWING
THAT YOU IN GOD? THANKS TO GOD, THIS BOOK WILL
EMPOWER YOU TO KNOW THE GOD IN YOU AS YOU KNOW*

YOURSELF. A MAN THAT KNOWS THE "ADAM" OF HIMSELF KNOWS MEN, BUT ALL MEN DON'T KNOW WHO MAN. AND IF "EVE" WAS THE FIRST WOMAN, WHAT IS THE REST? WELL, WHAT DOES THAT HAVE TO DO WITH HOW I CAN STOP USING DRUGS? EVERYTHING! BECAUSE EVERYTHING IN THIS WORLD IS ABOUT YOU, AND ONLY YOU AND NO ONE ELSE, BUT YOU! YOU ARE A MAN, GOD MADE YOU OF THE MIND, BUT THE DEVIL LIVES IN YOUR SUBCONSCIOUS MIND. THIS IS NOT TO SAY THAT A WOMAN DOESN'T HAVE A MIND, BUT IF YOU'RE A WOMAN, SATAN WILL ENSLAVE YOUR BODY. YOU WILL LOSE YOUR MIND, BODY, AND SOUL TRYING TO STAY HIGH AND FIND DRUGS. WHILE SHE'S SELLING HER MOST PRECIOUS JEWELS JUST TO GET HIGH. YOU KNOW YOU, AND YOU KNOW EXACTLY WHAT DRUGS MAKE YOU DO, SO DON'T YOU SAY THIS ISN'T TRUE, OTHERWISE, IT WILL BE THE DEVIL IN YOU.

YOU CAN'T RUN FROM DRUGS

YOU KNOW YOU CAN'T RUN FROM DRUGS AND YOU KNOW YOU DON'T NEED DRUGS. YOU KNOW DRUGS MAKE YOU AFRAID TO GO OUT THE HOUSE, BUT TODAY WHEN YOU USE DRUGS, YOU BECOME AFRAID IN YOUR HOUSE. WOE! YOU KNOW THE DEVIL IS IN DRUGS, BUT WHAT YOU DON'T KNOW IS THAT WHEN YOU USE DRUGS, THE DEVIL IS IN YOU. DON'T SAY THIS ISN'T TRUE, OTHERWISE, IT'S THE DEVIL IN YOU. THE DEVIL IN DRUGS BECOMES THE DEVIL IN YOU, BUT THE DEMON OF YOUR ADDICTION SAYS IT'S NOT TRUE. BUT THANKS BE TO GOD, YOU'RE FINALLY THROUGH, FOR YOU ARE READING A BOOK ABOUT YOU. AFTER THE READING OF THIS BOOK, YOU'LL BE THROUGH BECAUSE IN THESE PAGES YOU'LL SEE YOU. THIS BOOK WILL TALK TO YOU, COMFORT YOU, AND TEACH YOU WHAT TO DO, FOR IT'S ANOINTED BY GOD TO DELIVER YOU. IT IS NOT WHAT DRUGS HAVE DONE TO YOU AND NEVER WHAT DRUGS HAVE DONE FOR YOU, BUT THANKS BE TO GOD BECAUSE THROUGH DRUGS, YOU'VE FINALLY FOUND YOU!

HOLY BE HIS NAME! IT IS WRITTEN THAT IF YOU MAKE YOUR BED IN HELL HE'LL BE THERE WITH YOU (Psalm 139: 8), FOR YOU'RE YOU AREN'T YOU?

PUT GOD FIRST

PUT GOD FIRST IN WHATEVER YOU DO (Proverbs 3:6). YOU HAVE PUT YOURSELF AHEAD OF YOUR ADDICTION AND NOT GOD. YOU HAVE TAKEN GOD'S PLACE AND THE DRUGS HAVE DECEIVED YOU, FOR YOU'RE JUST AS WRONG ABOUT YOUR ADDICTION AS YOU'RE RIGHT ABOUT YOUR DAILY USAGES. AN ADDICTION LED TO GOD, BUT YOUR ADDICTION LED TO YOU. GOD HAS JUDGED YOU ON THE MERITS OF YOUR ADDICTION AS THE SIN OF YOU AND YOUR SIN IS NO DIFFERENT THAN ANYONE ELSE'S ADDICTION. ALL MORTAL SIN IS THE SAME. DO YOU NOT LOOK BACK AT OUR OWN FECAL MATTER BEFORE YOU FLUSH TO SEE WHAT CAME FROM YOU? HOW DO YOU STOP USING DRUGS? YOU MUST KNOW YOU! DO YOU KNOW YOU?

YOU ARE THE BLACK SHEEP

YOU ARE THE "BLACK SHEEP" OF THE FAMILY AND THE ONLY GOOD THING ABOUT IT IS THAT YOU KNOW IT. YOU HAVEN'T DONE A THING THAT YOU'RE SUPPOSED TO DO AND THIS YOU ALSO KNOW. WHAT YOU DON'T KNOW, BLACK SHEEP, IS THAT YOU'RE CAUGHT UP INTO SATAN'S TRIANGLE AND THE DEVIL'S DRUGS HAVE LED YOU TO PRAY. YOU'RE NOT PRAYING JUST BECAUSE IT'S THE RIGHT THING TO DO, YOU'RE PRAYING FOR YOUR LIFE BECAUSE THROUGH YOUR DRUG ADDICTION, THE DEVIL HAS SCARED THE LIVING HELL OUT OF YOU. WOE! MOMMA ALWAYS SAID THERE'S SOMETHING OUT THERE THAT WAS GOING TO GET YOU AND YOU FOUND OUT EXACTLY WHAT IT WAS—DRUGS. UNDERSTAND, YOU! THE GOOD SHEPARD HAS DOGS, BUT THESE DOGS ARE DOMESTIC ANIMALS THAT SNIPE AT THE BLACK SHEEPS FEET TO RUN THEM BACK INTO THE FLOCK. YOU HARD-HEAD, REBELLIOUS SHEEP! THE DEVIL HAS

DOGS! THESE VICIOUS DOGS OF CRACK, METH, HEROIN, PILLS, POWDER, PCP, ACID, AND OTHER MAN MADE DEMONIC DRUGS AREN'T FOUR LEGGED ANIMALS AS YOU MAY THINK. THEY ARE SUBCONSCIOUSLY THE PSYCHOLOGICAL BEAST THAT LIVES IN THE CHEMICAL WORLD OF YOUR DOGGISH DRUGS ADDICTION. ONLY YOU KNOW HOW FAR YOU ARE IN YOUR ADDICTION AND WHICH DOG IS SNIPPING AT YOUR FEET. CAN YOU HEAR THE DOGS COMING? YOU CAN SENSE IT IN YOUR SPIRIT AND WHEN YOU ARE GETTING HIGH, YOU HEAR THEM GROWLING, BUT IN YOUR LITTLE REST THEY ARE BARKING IN YOUR SLEEP.

WHAT KEEPS YOU ADDICTED

HOW TO STOP USING DRUGS DOES NOT COME FROM KNOWING WHAT DRUGS YOU'RE ADDICTED TO, BUT RATHER KNOWING WHAT KEEPS YOU ADDICTED TO IT. YOU CAN'T FOOL YOU, AND YOU KNOW EXACTLY WHAT KEEPS YOU ADDICTED TO DRUGS! DO YOU LIKE KINKY SEX? THEN KINKY SEX KEEPS YOU ADDICTED TO DRUGS. DO YOU LIKE BUTT-NAKED FUN? THEN HAVING BUTT-NAKED FUN KEEPS YOU ADDICTED TO DRUGS. THUS, YOU LIKE THE WAY DRUGS MAKE YOU FEEL? THEN THE WAY DRUGS MAKE YOU FEEL WILL KEEP YOU ADDICTED TO DRUGS, FOR REGARDLESS OF WHAT DRUGS YOU LIKE, YOUR ADDICTION LIES THEREIN WHAT YOU LIKE. PERHAPS, IF YOU TRY NOT LIKING WHAT YOU LIKE SO MUCH, YOU WOULD STOP USING DRUGS! A LOT OF PEOPLE THINK YOU CAN STOP USING DRUGS JUST LIKE THAT. THEY THINK THERE IS A QUICK FIX AND ALL YOU HAVE TO DO IS JUST SAY "NO", BUT THEY ARE NOT YOU! THIS BOOK IS ABOUT YOU, ONLY YOU, AND NO ONE ELSE, BUT YOU! THEY ARE NOT THE ONES ADDICTED TO DRUGS, FOR YOU SHOULD KNOW FOR YOURSELF THAT THEY TOO HAVE THEIR OWN ADDICTIONS! HAVE THEY HAVE CURED THEMSELVES JUST LIKE THAT? FOR YOU HAVE YOUR OWN DEMON ISN'T ONE DEVIL ENOUGH?

YOU ARE NOT ADDICTED

LEARNING HOW TO STOP USING DRUGS COMES FROM THE UNDERSTANDING THAT YOU ARE NOT ADDICTED TO A DRUG UNTIL YOU USE THE DRUG. THEN, AND ONLY THEN, WILL YOU BECOME ADDICTED TO THIS DRUG. YOU WILL REALIZE IT AT THAT PARTICULAR TIME AND ONLY DURING THAT PARTICULAR "HIGH" MOMENT. YOU ARE NOT ADDICTED TO THE DRUG ONCE YOU HAVE GONE HOME, EATEN, SLEPT, AND WOKEN UP THE NEXT DAY. THE HIGH IS OVER. THE CRAVING IS GONE AND THERE IS NO MORE ADDICTION, BUT YOU THINK YOUR ADDICTION STILL REMAINS EVEN WHEN YOU ARE NOT HIGH, HAVING CRAVINGS, OR HAVE NOT USED DRUGS. DO NOT CONFUSE YOUR USAGE OF A DRUG BY YOUR CRAVING FOR THE DRUG AS AN ADDICTION, OTHERWISE YOU WILL BECOME THE DRUG ITSELF.

DRUGS OF CHOICE

IF YOUR DRUG OF CHOICE IS CRACK, YOU'LL BECOME A CRACK HEAD; METH, A METH HEAD; AND IF IT'S POWDER, YOU'LL BECOME A JUNKIE. NOW, TELL ME, WHAT EFFECT DOES A DRUG HAVE ON YOU IF YOU HAVEN'T USE DRUGS? I'M TALKING, RIGHT NOW? EXACTLY, NONE! DRUGS HAVE NO POWER OVER YOU UNTIL YOU USE DRUGS AND WHEN YOU USE DRUGS, UNFORTUNATELY, YOU HAVE NO POWER OVER YOU. YOU HAVE ENTERED INTO THE SPIRITUAL WORLD OF YOUR SUBCONSCIOUS MIND. THE DEVIL HAS NOW POSSESSED YOU AND YOU ARE THEN ADDICTED TO THIS DRUG, AT THIS PARTICULAR TIME, AND ONLY DURING THIS PARTICULAR "HIGH" OF THE MOMENT. THIS IS BECAUSE YOU HAVE ALLOWED YOURSELF TO USE THE DRUG, FOR BY ALLOWING YOURSELF TO USE THE DRUG, EVERY STEP YOU TAKE IS DEADLY. BECAUSE IN THE SPIRITUAL WORLD OF YOUR SUBCONSCIOUS MIND, YOU ARE SURROUNDED BY DEATH. WOE! THE DEAD ARE AMONG YOU AND YOU SENSE IT IN YOUR SPIRIT, BUT KNOWING YOU, YOU'LL DO WHATEVER THE DRUGS WILL HAVE YOU TO DO. YOU WILL LOOK ON THE FLOOR FOR A

PIECE OF DOPE YOU THOUGHT YOU DROPPED WHEN ALL THE TIME IT WAS YOUR MIND YOU LOST! YES, IT WAS YOU YOU WERE LOOKING FOR. YOU WERE LOOKING FOR YOU.

DEVIL IN DRUGS BE DEVIL IN YOU

THE DRUGS HAVE YOU PEEPING OUT WINDOWS, RUNNING NAKED AROUND THE HOUSE, AND SEARCHING FOR MORE DRUGS AS IF YOU'RE HUNTING FOR HIDDEN TREASURES. THUS, YOU KNOW YOU, AND YOU KNOW EXACTLY WHAT DRUGS MAKE YOU DO. SO, DO NOT SAY THIS IS NOT TRUE OTHERWISE, IT WILL BE THE DEVIL IN YOU. THE DEVIL IN DRUGS BECOMES THE DEVIL IN YOU, BUT THE DEMON OF YOUR ADDICTION HAS SAID IT'S NOT TRUE. YET, YOU KNOW THE TRUTH, THAT WHEN YOU USE DRUGS, YOU ARE NOT YOU.YOU COULD'VE STOPPED USING DRUGS IF YOU WANTED TO. AS A MATTER OF FACT, YOU HAVE SLOWED DOWN. YOU HAVE EVEN QUIT EVERY NOW AND THEN, BUT RIGHT NOW, YOU JUST SNEAK AND DO YOU, AND ONLY YOU. DOES THIS SOUND LIKE YOU? WELL, THIS BOOK ABOUT YOU, ONLY YOU, AND NO ONE ELSE, BUT YOU. ALTHOUGH THE DEVIL IS SUBCONSCIOUSLY LISTENING AND HE HAS HEARD YOUR CONSCIOUS THOUGHTS, SATAN KNOWS WHAT YOU HAVE READ THUS FAR. YOUR SPIRITUAL EYES ARE OPENING, THE MIND'S EAR IS LISTENING, AND FOR THE FIRST TIME IN A LONG TIME, YOU CAN CLEARLY HEAR AND SEE YOUR OWN THOUGHTS. THIS IS THE FIRST STEP TO YOUR RECOVERY; HEARING AND SEEING YOUR GODLY THOUGHTS AS YOU CONTINUE TO READ AND UNDERSTAND THE DEMONIC ADDICTION OF YOU.

SATAN DECEPTIONS

HOW DO YOU TO STOP USING DRUGS? YOU MUST SEE YOU! THE DEVIL HAS CONFUSED AND DECEIVED YOU THROUGH YOUR DRUG USAGE. HE DOESN'T WANT YOU TO SEE YOU. THE FIRST THING HE TOOK WAS YOUR RESPECT. YET, YOU TRY HARD TO HIDE THE FACT THAT YOU USE DRUGS, BUT UNBEKNOWNST TO

YOU, YOU ARE LOOKING WORSE AND WORSE EACH DAY. THUS, THREE WEEKS LATER, YOU'RE A FULL-FLEDGED, RAGGEDY ADDICT WITH NO RESPECT FOR YOURSELF, AND RUNNING SCARED. THE RESPECT YOU ONCE HELD IS NOW GONE AND ALL YOU HAVE LEFT WILL SOON FOLLOW BECAUSE OF YOUR DEMONIC ADDICTION. THE DEVIL WANTS YOU TO THINK YOU'RE ADDICTED TO DRUGS JUST BECAUSE YOU USE DRUGS. HE WANTS YOU TO THINK YOU ARE A DRUGS ADDICT BECAUSE OF YOUR CRAVING FOR DRUGS AND IN HIS DECEPTION HE MAKES YOU DO ANYTHING FOR MORE DRUGS. THUS, HE MAKES YOU SUFFER FROM EXTREME FEAR EVERYTIME HE CAN DECEIVE YOU INTO USING DRUGS. DO YOU NOT SEE YOU?

THE DRUGS USE YOU

RIGHT NOW, PUT THIS BOOK DOWN IF YOU DON'T WANT TO KNOW HOW TO STOP USING DRUGS. OTHERWISE, UNDERSTAND! YOU HAVE NEVER USED DRUGS. THE DRUGS HAVE ALWAYS USED YOU. YOU THOUGHT YOU WERE USING DRUGS WHEN YOU WERE SHOOTING DRUGS. YOU THOUGHT YOU WERE USING DRUGS WHEN YOU WERE SMOKING DRUGS. AND YOU THOUGHT YOU WERE USING DRUGS WHEN YOU WERE SNORTING DRUGS AND POPPING PILLS, BUT ALL THE TIME THE DRUGS WERE USING YOU. IF THEY WERE NOT, HOW ELSE DID YOU GET HOOKED ON DRUGS? DO YOU BELIEVE YOU USED DRUGS RATHER THAN THE DRUGS USING YOU? YOU DIDN'T FIND DRUGS, DRUGS FOUND YOU. DRUGS HAVE NO HANDS, BUT YOUR HANDS. DRUGS HAVE NO LEGS, BUT YOUR LEGS. DRUGS HAVE NO FEET, BUT YOUR FEET. DRUGS HAVE NO THOUGHTS, BUT YOUR THOUGHTS SO, IF DRUGS ARE ON YOUR PERSON RIGHT NOW, WHO'S USING WHO? ARE YOU NOT THE ONE BEING USED BY THE DRUGS? OF COURSE, THE DEVIL GAVE YOU THE DRUGS, BUT DRUGS HAVE NO MIND, ONLY YOUR MIND. LOOK HOW SAD YOU'LL BE WHEN THE DEMONS DO NOT GET THEIR DRUGS.

GET OFF THE PITY POT!

THUS, GET OFF YOUR PITY POT, YOU! NO ONE CARES ABOUT YOUR SAD DEMON, BUT YOU! NOW, ANSWER YOURSELF THIS QUESTION. DO YOU USE DRUGS OR DO THE DRUGS USE YOU? THANKS BE TO GOD, FOR HE'LL PUT NOTHING UPON YOU THAT YOU CAN NOT HANDLE (1 Corinthians 10:13). OTHERWISE, YOU ARE SUBJECT TO LOSE YOUR MIND AND NOT FROM TAKING ANOTHER HIT, BUT BY THINKING YOU USED DRUGS WHEN ALL TIME THE DRUGS WERE USING YOU. RELAX. DO NOT JUST PONDER THIS FACT, BUT REMEMBER THAT THIS BOOK IS ABOUT YOU, ONLY YOU, AND NO ONE ELSE, BUT YOU. YET, YOU DOUBT EVERYTHING ABOUT YOU, BUT THAT'S JUST YOU, AND THAT'S WHY YOU STILL USE DRUGS TODAY. YOU DON'T LISTEN TO YOU.

YOU MUST LISTEN TO YOU

HOW DO YOU STOP USING DRUGS? YOU MUST LISTEN TO YOU, TALK TO YOU, AND BE NICE TO YOU. THANK GOD FOR BEING YOU. DO YOU NOT KNOW YOU'RE THE YOU? HOW STRANGE THIS MAY SEEM FOR YOU TO HAVE A CONVERSATION WITH YOU, BUT WHO ELSE CAN YOU TALK TO ABOUT YOUR DRUG ADDICTION BETTER THAN YOU? WHO ELSE KNOWS YOU BETTER THAN YOU KNOW YOU? WHO ELSE KNOWS WHAT YOU HAVE BEEN THROUGH OTHER THAN GOD AND YOU? OF COURSE, YOU KNOW THAT THERE ARE NO GOOD THINGS IN YOUR DRUG USAGE. YOU ARE TOTALLY AWARE OF WHAT DRUGS HAVE TAKEN FROM YOU, SO CERTAIN PEOPLE NEED TO MIND THEIR OWN BUSINESS. YOU WILL FIND THE GOD IN YOU, AND YOU WILL MAKE IT THROUGH. DOES THIS SOUND LIKE YOU? WELL, LISTENING TO YOU, SEEING YOU, AND UNDERSTANDING YOU ARE MAJOR STEPS TOWARDS YOUR DELIVERANCE. YOU ARE ABOUT TO SEE YOU.

GET UNDERSTANDING

THE BIBLE SAYS ABOVE ALL THINGS, GET AN UNDERSTANDING (Proverbs 4: 7). HOW CAN YOU UNDERSTAND SOMETHING IF YOU CAN NOT SEE IT? YOUR ADDICTION TO A DRUG IS SOMETHING THAT YOU KNOW, BUT CAN'T SEE. THANKS TO GOD, YOUR DEMONIC ADDICTION IS NOW BEING MANIFESTED UNTO YOU. A MAN IN THE DARK CAN'T SEE THE SHADOW THAT MOVES IN THE BLACK DARK OF THE NIGHT, BUT DID IT MOVE? WISDOM TEACHES YOU THAT IT MOVED, BUT UNDERSTANDING GIVES YOU THE KNOWLEDGE THAT IT CAN ONLY BE SEEN MOVING IN THE LIGHT. SURELY, THE SAME SHADOW YOU CAST IN LIGHT, YOU ALSO CAST IN DARKNESS. BUT YOU ARE RIGHT ABOUT YOU. CERTAIN PEOPLE WILL KEEP YOU ADDICTED TO DRUGS. FOR YOU KNOW THE ONES WHO CARE ABOUT YOU AND YOU KNOW THE ONES WHO WILL GIVE YOU DRUGS. FOR YOU KNOW THE ONES WHO WILL PRAY FOR YOU, AND YOU KNOW THE ONES WHO ARE SINCERE TO YOU, BUT YOU ALSO KNOW THE ONES WHO HOPE YOU NEVER GET OFF DRUGS. WELL, GUESS WHAT? THEY REALLY DON'T KNOW YOU AND AS A MATTER OF FACT, THEY DON'T EVEN KNOW THEMSELVES. FOR ONLY YOU KNOW YOU AND YOU WILL MAKE IT THROUGH BECAUSE YOUR ADDICTION IS NOT YOU!

ADDICTION LEADS TO GOD

HOW DO YOU STOP USING DRUGS? UNDERSTAND YOU! AN ADDICTION IS AN ADDICTION, BUT ALL ADDICTIONS LEAD TO GOD. WHETHER YOU'RE ADDICTED TO DRUGS, ALCOHOL, SEX, SLEEPING, EATING, STEALING, KILLING OR WHATEVER YOUR ADDICTION MIGHT BE. AN ADDICTION IS AN ADDICTION, BUT ALL ADDICTION LEADS TO GOD. THE BIBLE SAYS THAT ALL THINGS WORK TOGETHER FOR THE GOOD OF THOSE WHO LOVE GOD, TO THEM WHO ARE CALLED ACCORDING TO HIS PURPOSE. (Romans 8: 28). THUS, UNDERSTAND YOU! YOU HAVE BEEN CALLED ACCORDING TO GOD'S PURPOSE FOR YOU AND THERE IS NOTHING ABOUT YOU THAT HAS NOT BEEN

ORCHESTRATED BY GOD AND PERFECTLY PLANNED IN HEAVEN FIRST. YOUR ADDICTION TO DRUGS IS NO DIFFERENT THAN ANOTHER PERSON'S ADDICTION AS A SIN, FOR AN ADDICTION IS AN ADDICTION, BUT ALL ADDICTIONS ARE AS SIN. DO YOU NOT KNOW THAT YOU WOULD NOT HAVE FOUND GOD IF IT HAD NOT BEEN FOR YOUR SINFUL DRUG ADDICTION? HOW ELSE WOULD YOU HAVE FOUND GOD OTHER THEN THROUGH SIN? HAVEN'T YOU SUFFERED ENOUGH DRUGS IN YOUR SINFUL ADDICTION TO FIND GOD? HOW MANY TIMES HAVE YOU TRIED TO STOP USING DRUGS, BUT COULDN'T? HOW MANY PIPES HAVE YOU THROWN AWAY AND WENT BACK TO FIND, BUT COULDN'T? THEN WENT BACK TO FIND, BUT STILL COULDN'T! BUT THIS TIME, YOU SEARCHED UNTIL YOU FOUND THE DEVILISH THING JUST TO GET THAT LAST HIT. YOU KNEW THEN THAT YOU WERE POWERLESS TO DRUGS AND THAT YOU MUST RELY ON A POWER GREATER THAN YOU. THEN CAN'T YOU UNDERSTAND THAT YOUR ADDICTION TO DRUGS LED YOU TO GOD AND TO THE NEW FOUND CHRIST IN YOU?

DELIVERANCE FROM AN ADDICTION

FOR YOU ARE MORE CONTENT TODAY, "DESPITE WHAT PEOPLE MAY SAY OR THINK ABOUT YOU," THAN YOU HAVE EVER BEEN IN YOUR ENTIRE LIFE. PRAISE THE LORD! FOR ALTHOUGH YOUR ADDICTION HAS LEFT YOU BROKE, AND WITHOUT, YOU ARE JUST AS BLESSED. PRAISE THE LORD THAT GOD HAS DELIVERED YOU FROM THIS DEVILISH DOPE AND RELEASED YOUR SOUL FROM THE BOUNDS OF HELL. THAT YOU MAY HAVE A GOD PRAISING, FOOT STOMPING, HANDS WAVING, GOOD GOD SHOUTING TIME RIGHT NOW. HALLELUJAH! THANK YOU JESUS! MY LORD AND SAVIOR FOR FREEING ME FROM THE DRUG DENS OF SATAN. MY GOD! MY GOD! MY GOD! HALLELUJAH! THANK YOU JESUS, THANK YOU MY LORD, FOR THY DELIVERANCE! RIGHT THEN, YOU SHOULD HAVE FELT THE SPIRIT OF GOD REJOICING IN THE DELIVERANCE OF YOUR SOUL. IF SO, THE CHILLS FROM THE SPIRIT MEANT YOU WERE BEING DELIVERED BY GOD FROM THE DEMONS OF AN

ADDICTION. GOD HAS CAST YOUR ADDICTION INTO THE SEA OF FORGETFULNESS (Micah 7:18-19) (Psalm 103:12). ALL THAT SATAN HAS TAKEN FROM YOU SHALL BE RESTORED SEVEN FOLD TIMES THAT WHICH HE HAS TAKEN, THUS SAITH THE LORD! YOUR ADDICTION TO DRUGS WAS LIKE YOUR LIFE SCRIPT THAT GOD WROTE FOR YOU TO FIND THE GOD IN YOU. "THE EARTH IS THE LORD'S AND THE FULLNESS THEREOF, AND HE GIVETH IT TO WHOMSOEVER HE PLEASES" (1 Corinthians 10: 26). THANKS BE TO GOD YOU DON'T HAVE TO DEPEND ON YOU, OTHERWISE YOU WOULD STILL BE USING DRUGS. YOU MAY THINK YOU DELIVERED YOU AND NOT GOD. YET, YOU ARE NOT KEEPING YOURSELF ALIVE AND YOU HAVE NO POWER OVER LIFE AND DEATH. YOU KNOW HAD IT NOT BEEN FOR GOD DURING THE TIMES YOU WERE BOOZING AND USING, YOU WOULD HAVE BEEN DEAD, DON'T YOU? PRAISE THE LORD, BLACK SHEEP, THE WOOL IS COMING OFF AND NOW YOU KNOW THE GOD IN YOU AS THE SHEARER OF YOUR ADDICTION.

THE GOD IN YOU

HOW DO YOU STOP USING DRUGS? IT DEPENDS ON YOU KNOWING THE GOD IN YOU FOR YOURSELF. NO ONE ELSE CAN KNOW GOD FOR YOU. NO ONE ELSE CAN STOP USING DRUGS FOR YOU. NO ONE ELSE CAN STOP YOU FROM USING DRUGS, BUT THE GOD IN YOU AND YOU IN GOD. YOU'VE GOT TO HAVE AN INTERPERSONAL RELATIONSHIP WITH GOD THROUGH HIS SON CHRIST JESUS (John 14:6). OTHERWISE, YOU'LL NEVER KNOW YOU AND FOREVER BE ADDICTED TO DRUGS. THIS, YOU ALREADY KNOW, BUT WHAT YOU DON'T KNOW, BLACK SHEEP, IS EVEN THE PRODIGAL SON KNEW WHEN TO GO BACK HOME (Luke 15:11-32). YOU ARE LOST FROM THE FATHER, DYING FROM DRUGS, AND HAVE FORGOTTEN YOUR WAY BACK HOME. WHAT ABOUT YOU MY SISTER? AREN'T YOU SO HAPPY YOU HAVE FOUND THE LORD?! UNDERSTAND YOU! MONEY IS A MOTIVATING FORCE THAT MAKES YOU GET OUT OF YOUR BED LATE AT NIGHT, EARLY IN THE MORNING, OR ANY TIME DURING THE DAY, AND GO TO WORK. YOUR ADDICTION TO DRUGS ARE MOTIVATING FORCES

*THAT MAKE YOU SEEK GOD'S DELIVERANCE. MAN'S INFIRMITY IS
GOD'S OPPORTUNITY (2 Corinthians 1:8) (Psalm 77:2-4). GOD
KNOWS THAT YOU'RE POWERLESS TO DRUGS, AND HE ALSO
KNOWS WHETHER OR NOT YOU WANT TO STOP USING DRUGS.
THUS, DON'T PLAY WITH GOD IN YOUR ADDICTION! FOR HE'LL
DESTROY YOU! HE KNOWS YOU BETTER THAN YOU KNOW YOU!*

YOU IN GOD

*HOW TO STOP USING DRUGS COMES FROM THE DIVINE
KNOWLEDGE OF GOD WITHIN YOU. YOUR UNDERSTANDING OF
THE HOLY ONE WILL TAKE THE TASTE OF DRUGS COMPLETELY
OUT OF YOUR MOUTH. BLACK SHEEP, YOU ARE THE SEED AND
A DIRECT DESCENDANT OF THE PRODIGAL SON WHO ATE
WITH THE SWINES (Luke 15: 11-32). YOU ARE THE SAME
PERSON WHO PEOPLE HATED TO SEE COMING BECAUSE IN
YOUR ADDICTION THEY DIDN'T HAVE ANYTHING TO GIVE YOU.
PERHAPS, THE ONLY DIFFERENCE BETWEEN NOW AND THEN,
AND YOU AND HIM, IS THAT IN THE OLD DAYS HE ATE WITH
THE HOGS, BUT AT THIS TIME, YOU EAT WITH THE DOGS. YET,
AS HE WAS, SO ARE YOU A CHOSEN VESSEL OF GOD. YOU HAVE
SQUANDERED YOUR PORTION OF PROSPERITY ON DRUGS,
WINE, GOOD TIMES, AND FINE WOMEN. THUS, THE SAME AS
HIM, BUT NOW THEY'RE ALL GONE. LEAVING YOU BEHIND AS A
PROFESSIONAL BEGGAR, DRUG ADDICT, AND A VAGABOND.
WOE! THE SAME PEOPLE THAT HELPED HIM TO BECOME
BROKE, HELPED YOU TO BECOME BROKE. THEY LAUGHED AT
HIM, LIKE THEY LAUGH AT YOU. THEY DON'T WANT TO BE
AROUND HIM ANYMORE THAN THEY WANT TO BE AROUND
YOU, FOR NO MAN GAVE UNTO HIM BREAD (Luke 15: 16). WOE!*

SCAB DEMONS

*YOU'RE LIKE A WALKING CRACKHEAD TO THEM, NOTHING
MORE THAN THE NEIGHBORHOOD DRUG ADDICT. YOU CARRY
THE DEVIL'S HORN (pipe) WHEREVER YOU GO AND YOU TREAT*

THE FIRE-BREATHING DEMON BETTER THAN YOU DO YOURSELF. YOU LOVE IT MORE THAN YOU DO YOURELF AND YOU DEPEND ON IT FOR WHATEVER YOU DO. THUS, YOU LOVE IT MORE THAN YOU DO GOD, BUT NOW YOU WANT TO STICK YOURSELF WITH A NEEDLE AND FEED THE DEVIL'S POISION THROUGH YOUR VEINS. ARE YOU INSANE? HAVE YOU LOST YOUR MIND? YOU SEEK THE ULTIMATE HIGH, WHICH IS DEATH. YET, YOU DIE EVERY TIME YOU GO TO SLEEP. NODDING WITH THE SNAKE-BITTEN NEEDLE DANGLING FROM YOUR ARM PIT, A DEMONIC SCAB HAS ATTACHED ITSELF TO THE PIT OF YOUR ARM. NO MATTER IF IT IS DAY OR NIGHT OR WHETHER IT RAINS, SLEETS OR SNOWS, YOU WILL ROB, STEAL, AND KILL TO FEED THE ALIEN SCAB. IT GETS BIGGER AND MORE DEMANDING FOR DRUGS EACH DAY AND AFTER EVERY HIT. YOU DON'T KNOW THIS, BUT YOU'RE FEEDING A SCAB DEMON THAT HAS ATTACHED ITSELF TO THE PIT OF YOUR ARM AND NOT YOUR VEIN. YOU WERE GIVEN AN ILLUSION BY SATAN THAT YOU WERE HITTING THE RIGHT VEIN, BUT ALL THE TIME YOU WERE BEING DECEIVED. YOU ARE FEEDING THAT DEMONIC SCAB THAT HAS ATTACHED ITSELF TO YOUR VEIN. THE UGLY DEMON ATTACHES ITSELF LIKE A LEECH AND SUCKS THE LIFE OUT OF YOU THROUGH A NEEDLE OF DOPE. WOE!

SATAN THE MASTER OF ILLUSION

YOU FEEL LIKE YOU'VE BEEN CHEATED BY THE DEVIL AND YOU HAVE BECAUSE SATAN IS THE MASTER OF ILLUSIONS. YOU'RE EXPERIENCING AN ILLUSION, BUT THE DEMON ATTACHED TO YOUR ARM IS THE ONE GETTING FED AND USING DRUGS. EVEN WHILE YOU ARE NODDING, SLEEPING, AND HALF DEAD, SCAB DEMONS ATTACH THEMSELVES TO THE BODY. THEY ARE VISIBLE TO THE EYES, BUT THEY IS SOME PUSS AND BLOODY SITES. YOU'LL GET SICK JUST BY LOOKING AT THEM DURING FEEDING TIME. THE OOZING, YELLOWISH PUSS, BLEEDING, MIXED WITH THE THICK MILKY OPEN WOUND LOOKING SUBSTANCES IS EVEN MORE GROSS. WOE! SCAB DEMONS ARE THE WORST DEMONS IN THE CHEMICAL WORLD OF A DRUG

ADDICTION, FOR THEY ATTACH THEMSELVES TO THE BODY. THEY FOLLOW THE NEEDLE POINT AND THEY STICK TO THAT SPOT, BUT THEY LEAVE TRACKS. THEY WILL KEEP YOU BEGGING, BORROWING, AND HANGING ON TO THE NEEDLES OF LIFE AS THE ILLUSION STILL STANDS THAT YOU ARE HITTING THE RIGHT VEIN. SATAN IS PUTTING YOU INTO A DEEPER SLEEP. DO YOU BELIEVE THAT GOD CAN STOP THEM IN THEIR TRACKS?

DELIVERANCE FROM SCAB DEMON

THUS, SAITH THE LORD, TAKE THE SYRINGE AFTER THE USAGE OF YOUR FAVORITE DRUG OF CHOICE AND BURY IT DEEP INTO THE EARTH IN THE NAME OF THE FATHER, THE SON, AND THE HOLY GHOST. YOU HAVE DISPOSED OF THE NEEDLES IN TRASH CANS, DITCHES, ALLEY WAYS, AND EVERY OTHER PLACE YOU HAVE HIT ON EARTH, BUT YOU HAVE NEVER BURIED YOUR ADDICTION AS IN THE LORD (Matthew 11:28). FOR IN DOING SO, IN THE NAME OF THE FATHER, THE SON, AND THE HOLY GHOST, YOUR ADDICTION WILL NO LONGER BE BURIED IN YOU, BUT BE BURIED WITHIN THE BODY OF CHRIST. THAT IS IF CHRIST IS IN YOU (Romans 8:9). BY BURYING YOUR ADDICTION IN EARTH, IT BECAME A SYMBOLIC REPRESENTATION OF YOUR FAITH THAT GOD WILL DELIVER YOU FROM DRUGS. FOR THAT WHICH IS BURIED IN EARTH SHALL BE COVERED BY DIRT AND THE DEEPER IT'S BURIED, THE HARDER WILL IT BE TO FIND OR DIG BACK UP. THE SAME SHOULD BE OF YOUR ADDICTION AS IT BURIED IN THE LORD (Matthew 11: 28-30). YOU ARE OF THE EARTH AND DUST YOU ARE, AND DUST SHALL YOU RETURN (Genesis 3:19). YOUR ADDICTION, WHICH YOU BURIED IN CHRIST, SHALL ALSO DIE IN CHRIST. THAT WHICH SHALL RISE IN CHRIST SHALL BE YOU (1 Corinthians 15: 14) (Hebrews 6: 1-2). THUS, SAITH THE LORD! YOUR DEMONIC ADDICTION WILL NO LONGER BE BURIED WITHIN YOU, BUT HENCE FORTH INTO THE BODY OF THE LORD.

SUBMISSIVE TO OBEDIENCE

YOU MUST PRAY AND FAST THREE DAYS AFTER YOU BURY YOUR ADDICTION IN THE LORD. IN DOING SO, YOU WILL HAVE HUMBLED YOURSELF UNTO YOUR SALVATION, FOR YOU WILL HAVE SHOWN GOD THAT YOU WERE ADDICTED TO DRUGS THROUGH THE NEEDLE AND YOU WERE TIRED OF USING DRUGS. YOUR SINCERE EFFORTS TO BURY YOUR ADDICTION AND STOP USING DRUGS WILL DELIVER YOU FROM THAT POINT ON BECAUSE YOU HAVE BECOME SUBMISSIVE TO THE OBEDIENCE OF GOD. YOU HAVE DONE EXACTLY WHAT GOD HAS ALWAYS WANTED YOU TO DO, TO CALL ON THE LORD SO THAT HE CAN DELIVER YOU. YOUR FAITH SHALL MAKE YOU WHOLE, THUS SAITH THE LORD. YOU MUST HAVE FAITH THAT GOD WILL DELIVER YOU FROM DRUGS, OTHERWISE, FAITH WITHOUT WORKS IS DEAD (James 2: 17).

A JUST MAN

THE BIBLE SAYS THAT A JUST MAN WILL FALL SEVEN TIMES AND RISE, BUT THE WICKED SHALL FALL INTO MISCHIEF (Proverbs 24:16). HOW MANY OF YOUR ADDICTED FRIENDS ARE STILL OUT THERE DRUGGING, STRUNG OUT, OR DEAD? THANK GOD YOU DIDN'T FALL INTO MISCHIEF BECAUSE YOU WERE NOT WICKED. YOU ARE THE BLACK SHEEP, BUT YOU HAVE ALWAYS KNOWN GOD'S NAME AND GOD HAS ALWAYS KNOWN YOU. WHAT? KNOW YOU NOT, BLACK SHEEP, THAT YOU WERE AS GOD? THUS, DID GOD NOT CREATE YOU IN HIS OWN IMAGE (Genesis 1: 26)? FOR IN THE IMAGE OF GOD, HE MADE MAN AND A MAN IS A MAN FROM HIS SHOULDERS UP. GOD MADE MAN UPRIGHT AND OF THE MIND, BUT MIND YOU THERE ARE WOMEN WHO HAVE MORE SENSE IN THREE SECONDS THAN SOME MEN HAVE IN THIRTY MINUTES. THERE ARE WOMEN WHO CAN OUT THINK A MAN, OUT TALK A MAN, AND EVEN WHIP A MAN. BUT THE WOMAN WHO USES DRUGS SUFFERS GREATER ON DRUGS THAN THAT OF THE MAN. SATAN PROSTITUTES HER BODY IN SUPPORT OF HER DRUG ADDICTION TO THE DEGRADATION OF HERSELF, HER FAMILY, AND HER FRIENDS. WOE!

OH DESPICABLE YOU!

DRUGS DOESN'T DISCRIMINATE AND JUST LIKE THE DEVIL, DRUGS HAVE NO MORE RESPECT FOR THE NAKED MAN RUNNING DOWN THE STREET LOSING HIS MIND, THAN IT DOES FOR THE POOR, HELPLESS, HUNGRY CHILDREN LEFT ALONE IN A COLD, DARK, FREEZING HOUSE (Matthew 19: 14). DRUGS ARE EVIL AND ANYTHING THAT'S EVIL, WICKED, AND NO GOOD BELONGS TO THE DEVIL. NOW, WHAT ABOUT YOU? DO YOU BELONG TO GOD OR DO YOU BELONG TO THE DEVIL? KNOW YOU NOT WHO YOU BELONG TO? YOU BELONG TO GOD NOT THE DEVIL. YET, "YOU ARE WHICHEVER YOU ARE." THE LACK OF YOUR UNDERSTANDING MAKES YOU WHO YOU ARE, OH DESPICABLE YOU! YOU WERE THE SAME PERSON WHO TOLD MY CHILDREN TO GO HOME WHEN THEY NEEDED TO COME IN OUT THE COLD RAIN. YOU KNOW I KNOW YOU AND YOU KNOW I WAS ON ONE (High). YOU KNEW THEY WERE WITHOUT SHELTER. YOU FED MY CHILDREN NO GOOD STORIES OF ME WHILE YOU GAVE YOURS BREAD, BUT THEN YOU SAY YOU'RE MY SISTER? WHEN I WAS ON ONE, YOU STRIPPED ME NAKED AND USED MY BODY TO BECOME THE OBJECT OF YOUR DESIRES, BUT YOU SAY YOU'RE MY BROTHER?

THE WILES AND WOES OF EVE!

I AM EVE "THE MOTHER OF ALL LIVING THINGS" (Genesis 3:20)! YET, YOU MAKE ME A DRUG ADDICT AND A WHORE! I AM YOUR DAUGHTER, COULD BE YOUR MOTHER, OR EVEN YOUR SISTER, BUT YOU KNOW NOT WHO I AM, FOR YOU KNOW NOT YOURSELF, ADAM (1 Corinthians 15:45)! THUS, YOU WERE MY DADDY, MAN. GOD IS MY FATHER! BUT WHERE'S MY MOTHER? ABBA FATHER, WHAT HORRIBLE FATE HAS BECOME MY TRANSGRESSIONS SINCE MY FALL FROM THE GARDEN OF EDEN (Genesis 3:2)? TODAY, MY EARTHLY DADDY DISOWNS ME, MY FAMILY DOESN'T LOVE ME, AND ALL I HAVE ARE MY MOTHER'S PRAYERS, BUT WHERE'S MY POOR MOTHER? OH MOMMA, PLEASE! HELP ME GRANDMOTHER. O LORD, SAVE ME FROM THIS HORRIBLE FATE I HAVE BESTOWED UPON MYSELF (Genesis 3:13)!

CHILDREN FORSAKEN FOR DRUGS

I HAVE FORSAKEN MY CHILDREN FOR DRUGS. AS OF THIS DAY, I AM JUST AS LOST TO THE WORLD SAME AS THE INNOCENT LIVES I HAVE FORSAKEN. FOR SHORT EVIL DAYS AND LONG DARK, DEADLY NIGHTS, I STAND IDLING ON STREET CORNERS IN MY DESPERATE SEARCH FOR DRUGS. YET, I FIND NO REST FOR MY WEARY SOUL AND I LIVE BY THE ROCK OF MY PIPE, FOR THE CHILDREN'S BREAD GOES UNTO THE DOGS (Mark 7:27). THE BIBLE SAYS MY GOD IS A ROCK (2 Samuel 22:3), BUT THE DEMONS OF MY ADDICTION HAVE MADE MY PIPE BECOME MY GOD. WOE! WHEN YOU SEE ME, YOU DON'T SEE ME. OUT OF YOUR HATRED FOR ME, YOU LOOK THE OTHER WAY. YET, YOU DON'T KNOW MY PAINS NOR DO YOU UNDERSTAND MY SORROWS. YOU ACT AS IF I HAVE NO REGRETS, FOR YOU ONLY SEE MY ADDICTION, MY WEAKNESS, WHAT I AM, AND WHAT I HAVE BECOME, BUT YOU DON'T SEE ME! WHAT'S WRONG WITH YOU? YOU'RE NOT THE ONE ADDICTED TO DRUGS!

SPIDER WEB OF AN ADDICTION

DO YOU NOT SEE I'M LIKE A FLY CAUGHT IN THE WEB OF A SPIDER? I AM AT THE MERCY OF THE SPIDER AS I AM A PRISONER IN THE DRUG DENS OF SATAN? LORD, HAVE MERCY ON THEIR BLIND SOULS! DO YOU THINK I LIKE BEING PROSTITUTED BY MY DEMONIC ADDICTION BEFORE YOU? DO YOU THINK I LIKE BEING STRIPPED NAKED AND ABUSED UNDER THE SWEAT OF WHOREMONGERING MEN? YOU MUST THINK I LIKE DOING THE THINGS I DO; THE THINGS YOU SEE ME DO, AND THE THINGS YOU KNOW I DO! YOU MUST THINK IT IS MY WILL TO BE AS I AM; TO DO AS I DO, AND TO LIVE AND DIE GETTING HIGH WITH YOU! YOU MUST THINK IT IS MY WILL NOT TO BE ABLE TO EAT, SLEEP, OR NOT BE ABLE TO GET OUT THESE DRUGS INFESTED STREETS! DO YOU NOT LOVE ME ENOUGH TO HELP SAVE MY SOUL? TAKE ME BY FORCE, I BEG YOU, AGAINST MY WILL. LEAD ME UNTO THE ROCK OF MY SALVATION (Psalm 62:6)! YOU KNOW ME AS I AM; THE SISTER,

DAUGHTER, AND MOTHER OF ALL LIVING THINGS! YET, YOU HAVE FORGOTTEN WHO I AM AS EVE AND AS ADAM THROUGH TIME AND DRUGS HAVE MADE ME FORGET MYSELF. MAY THE LORD HAVE MERCY ON HER SOUL. YOU KNEW THE WOMAN HAD ENOUGH PROBLEMS BEFORE YOU TALKED HER INTO USING DRUGS. YOU NEW THIS BEFORE YOU SEDUCED HER MIND WITH DRUGS AND ENJOYED HER BODY WITH THE FIERY TONGUE OF YOUR DEMONIC ADDICTION.

BEWARE OF OTHER'S ADDICTIONS.

HOW DO YOU STOP USING DRUGS? YOU MUST KNOW WHO TO TALK AND LISTEN TO OTHER THAN YOURSELF. HALF YOUR TROUBLES COME FROM SOMEONE OTHER THAN YOU AND THE OTHER HALF COME FROM YOU AND WHAT YOU DO. YET, YOU HAVE NEVER GOTTEN INTO TROUBLE FOR WHAT YOU SHOULD HAVE DONE. AND YOU KNOW EXACTLY WHAT YOU SHOULD HAVE DONE. BUT YOU EXPECT THINGS TO GET BETTER WITH THEM BEING UNDONE. YOU MUST GO BACK INTO THE FLOCK AND ASK GOD TO DELIVER YOU FROM DRUGS. GOD WILL DELIVER YOU UPON HEARING FROM YOU AND YOU DON'T HAVE TO BE IN CHURCH TO BE OF THE CHURCH. THE CHURCH IS IN YOUR HEART. YOU MUST GO BACK INTO THE CHURCH OF YOUR HEART, CHANGE YOUR WICKED WAYS (2 Chronicles 7: 14), AND ASK GOD TO DELIVER YOU. THE BIBLE SAYS "TRUST IN THE LORD WITH ALL THINE HEART, AND LEAN NOT UNTO THINE OWN UNDERSTANDING. IN ALL THY WAYS ACKNOWLEDGE HIM, AND HE SHALL DIRECT THY PATH (Proverbs 3: 5- 6)."

CROSS ROAD OF AN ADDICTION

YOU MUST GO BACK TO THE CROSS ROAD OF YOUR ADDICTION AND ASK GOD TO DIRECT YOUR PATH. YOUR OLD PATH WAS FILLED WITH UNRIGHTEOUNESS AND YOU WERE ARROGANT IN GOD'S EYE. YET, IT WAS YOUR DOUBLE-DOG-DARE YOU ATTITUTE THAT LED TO YOUR ADDICTION. YOU THOUGHT YOU

COULD TRY ANYTHING ONCE, BUT GOD HAD TO SHOW YOU THAT SOMETIMES ONCE IS ALL IT TAKE. THUS, AFTER YOUR FIRST HIT, YOU WERE HOOKED ON DRUGS AND EVER SINCE THEN YOU BEEN FIGHTING THE DEMON OF YOUR ADDICTION. HOWEVER, HUMILIATION COMES BEFORE HONOR (Proverbs 15:33) AND NOW, BLACK SHEEP, YOU MUST SEEK CHRIST TO BE DELIVERED WITH HONORS. YOU HAVE TURNED THE CORNER OF PRAYERS AND GOT OFF THE STRAIGHT AND NARROW ROAD THAT WAS IN THE HEART OF YOUR BLESSING. YOU WENT RIGHT BY THE CHURCH NOT KNOWING YOU ARE THE CHURCH AND YOU PROBABLY HAVE FORGOTTEN HOW TO PRAY.

YOUR PRAYERS

HOW DO YOU STOP USING DRUGS? YOU MUST PRAY, FAST, AND PRESS YOUR WAY THROUGH YOUR ADDICTION (Matthew 6:16-18) BECAUSE YOU CAN'T BE DELIVERED FROM DRUGS WITHOUT PRAYERS. YOUR PRAYERS COME FROM GOD IN YOU AND GOD ANSWERS THE PRAYERS THAT COME FROM YOU IN GOD. YES, YOU'RE IN GOD AS GOD IN YOU. IF NOT, HOW ELSE CAN YOU PRAY IF GOD BE NOT IN YOU? THE FACT THAT YOU PRAY MEANS GOD IS IN YOU. DO YOU THINK IF THE DEVIL WAS IN YOU, HE WOULD PRAY TO GOD? YOU HAVE BEEN DECEIVED BY YOUR DEMONIC ADDICTION. NOW, GET DOWN ON YOUR KNEES AND PRAY, BECAUSE THE LORD FORGIVES YOU, BUT MAKE HASTE! GOD HASN'T FORGOTTEN ABOUT YOU, BUT JUST LIKE DRUGS, YOU'RE NOT THROUGH. DO YOU REMEMBER THE YOUNG WOMAN YOU INTRODUCED TO DRUGS? SHE WAS THE PRIDE OF HER FAMILY AND WAS LOVED AND RESPECTED BY THEM ALL. HAVE YOU NOT SEEN HER TODAY? HER SOFT DELICATE SKIN IS ABOUT AS DRY AND CRACKED AS THE EARTH. MY LORD, HER ONCE LOVELY FACE IS LIKE A STRANGER TO HER OWN FAMILY AND HER POOR WRETCHED BODY IS BEING EATEN AWAY BY THE DOGS OF HER DEMONIC ADDICTION. GOOD GOD ALMIGHTY! HAVE YOU REPENTED FOR HER YET? WHY NOT?!

REPENT!

HOW DO YOU STOP USING DRUGS? YOU MUST REPENT FOR YOUR TRANSGRESSIONS AND ASK GOD THROUGH CHRIST TO FORGIVE YOUR SINS (Psalm 103: 12) (1 John 1:9). THE YOUNG WOMAN IS LOST IN THE WORLD OF SIN AND LEST SHE SEEK THE LORD, SHE WILL FOREVER BE LOST IN HER ADDICTION. TODAY, SHE BLINDLY WALKS BACK AND FORTH, TO AND FROM, AND UP AND DOWN THE EARTH AS SHE TRAVELS THE ROUTE OF THE DEVIL (Job 1:7). YET, SHE IS STILL SOMEBODY'S DAUGHTER, BUT BECAUSE OF YOU, HER DRUG ADDICTION, AND UNGODLY WAYS SHE HAS BEEN DISOWNED AND FORSAKEN BY FAMILY AND FRIENDS. WOE! HAVE YOU REPENTED FOR INTRODUCING HER TO DRUGS? WHY NOT? HER SINS ARE YET UPON YOU. DO YOU NOT THINK YOU'RE RESPONSIBLE FOR HER ADDICTION? UNDERSTAND YOU! ALTHOUGH YOU INTRODUCED HER TO DRUGS, YOU ARE NOT THE ONE RESPONSIBLE FOR HER ADDICTION, FOR YOU ARE ONLY RESPONSIBLE FOR YOUR REACTION TO THE THINGS IN THIS LIFE THAT HAPPEN TO YOU. WHO YOU ARE OR WHAT YOU DO DOESN'T MEAN THAT YOU KNOW YOU. THEREFORE, YOU ARE ONLY A SHADOW OF YESTERDAY (Job 8:9) AND YOU KNOW NOT THAT WHICH IS TO HAPPEN, BUT ONLY THAT WHICH HAS ALREADY PASSED. AS A MATTER OF FACT, YOU KNEW AHEAD OF TIME YOU THAT WOULD BE READING THIS BOOK ABOUT "HOW TO STOP USING DRUGS" OR HAS THIS ALSO PASSED? HAVE YOU FORGOTTEN THAT GOD CREATED HER, AS HE CREATED YOU OR DID YOU CREATE YOU? HAD YOU CREATED YOU, WOULD YOU USE DRUGS AS YOU DO? SURELY, YOU WOULD HAVE CREATED YOU MUCH MORE PERFECTLY WOULDN'T YOU?

MAN'S GOING OF THE LORD

MAN'S GOINGS ARE OF THE LORD. HOW, THEN, CAN A MAN UNDERSTAND HIS OWN WAY (Proverbs 20: 24)? FOR IN THIS LIFE, YOU CAN'T UNDERSTAND YOUR OWN WAY. THEREFORE, HOW CAN YOU UNDERSTAND YOUR ADDICTION? YOU THOUGHT YOU HAD A CHOICE WHEN YOU GOT HOOKED ON

DRUGS, DIDN'T YOU? YOU THOUGHT IT WAS YOU WHO HOOKED HER ON DRUGS, DIDN'T YOU? NOW YOU THINK YOU ALONE CAN GET OFF DRUGS, DON'T YOU? YOU ARE WRONG ABOUT YOU; THIS THING IS BIGGER THAN YOU. WHAT? IT'S NOT?! THEN, CAN YOU CONTROL EVIL? OF COURSE NOT! DRUGS ARE EVIL, WICKED, AND NO GOOD. ARE YOU EVIL, WICKED, AND, NO GOOD? OF COURSE NOT! THEREFORE, THE YOUNG WOMAN BEING HOOKED ON DRUGS WASN'T BY YOUR CREATION OF EVIL, BUT BY GOD'S LIFE CREATION OF YOU.

GOD CREATION OF YOU

YOU ARE YOU AREN'T YOU? DO YOU NOT UNDERSTAND SHE WAS CREATED BY GOD, AND NOT BY YOU?! THE DRUGS HAVE DECEIVED YOU. YOU THINK SHE WAS CREATED BY YOU, AND NOT BY GOD. YET, GOD CREATED HER AS HE CREATED YOU. THEREFORE, HOW CAN YOU BE RESPONSIBLE FOR HER BEING ON DRUGS WHEN YOU ARE NOT RESPONSIBLE FOR YOU? DO YOU NOT UNDERSTAND THAT GOD CREATED YOU TO DO WHATEVER YOU DO AND GO THROUGH WHATEVER YOU GO THROUGH IN ORDER FOR YOU TO FIND YOU?! YOU DIDN'T CREATE YOU. THERE ARE MANY OF YOU, AND YOU'RE NOT THE ONLY YOU. YET, MANY OF YOU SPEND A LIFETIME IN SEARCH OF YOU, BUT NEVER GO THROUGH THE DOORS OF YOUR ADDICTION TO FIND THE GOD IN YOU, BUT YOU FOUND GOD IN YOU, AND YOU MADE IT THROUGH. HOW WONDERFUL IT MUST BE TO HAVE FOUND GOD IN YOU! DO YOU THINK EVERYBODY IS ON DRUGS? DO YOU THINK EVERYBODY IS AN ALCOHOLIC? THEY MUST FIND THEMSELVES. THEY ARE NOT YOU! THIS BOOK IS ABOUT YOU, ONLY YOU, AND NO ONE ELSE BUT YOU! DO YOU HAVE A PROBLEM WITH THE ADDICTION THAT GOD HAS USED IN ORDER FOR YOU TO FIND YOU? HAVEN'T YOU FOUND YOU?! WHY NOT? YOU'RE TALKING TO YOU. WHAT? YOU DON'T KNOW YOU'RE TALKING TO YOU? YOU MUST THINK IT IS CRAZY TO ACCEPT THIS TRUTH, BUT WHAT HAVE YOU READ ABOUT YOUR ADDICTION THAT WASN'T YOU?

REPENT!

HOW DO YOU STOP USING DRUGS? YOU MUST REPENT (Acts 2:38-39) FOR WHATEVER WRONG YOU DID AND WILL DO. IF YOU DO THE RIGHT THINGS, GOD IS WITH YOU. DRUGS ARE EVIL AND YOU CAN NOT CONTROL SOMETHING THAT IS EVIL. WHAT CAN YOU DO WITH SOMETHING THAT'S EVIL EXCEPT PRAY? HELP US LORD, FOR AT BEDTIME, DO YOU NOT PRAY TO GOD TO PROTECT YOU FROM EVIL?! (Matthew 6:9-13) YOU DON'T?! THEN HURRY UP, GET BACK DOWN ON YOUR KNEES, AND QUICKLY PRAY TO GOD TO PROTECT YOU FROM EVIL. WHY? BECAUSE GOD CREATED EVIL! THE SAME AS HE CREATED YOU (Isaiah 45:7) (Genesis 1: 26-28). DO YOU LIKE BEING EVIL WHEN YOU HAVE USED DRUGS? HOW CAN YOU NOT BE EVIL WHEN YOU HAVE USED SOMETHING THAT IS EVIL? WHEN YOU FART, CAN YOU NOT SMELL IT WITH THE NOSE? THEN HOW CAN YOU CONTROL SOMETHING THAT YOU DID NOT CREATE? NOW, SINCE YOU DIDN'T CREATE EVIL, NOR CAN YOU CONTROL EVIL, WHO THEN CAN CONTROL EVIL OTHER THAN YOU? EXACTLY! NOW, QUICKLY GET BACK DOWN ON YOUR KNEES, PRAY, AND ASK GOD TO HAVE MERCY ON YOU. YOU HAVE KNOWN GOD'S NAME AND BY YOU KNOWING HIS NAME, GOD HAS TAKEN THE TASTE FOR DRUGS OFF THE TIP OF YOUR TONGUE. AND THE CRAVING FOR DRUGS COMPLETELY OUT OF YOUR MIND, FOR HE IS A GOOD GOD. HOLY BE HIS NAME. YOU MUST UNDERSTAND THE HOLINESS OF GOD TO BE DELIVERED FROM THE DEMON IN YOUR ADDICTION. YOUR KNOWLEDGE OF THE GOD IN YOU GIVE YOU ABSOLUTE POWER OVER ALL EVIL. AMEN! YOU HAVE WEATHERED THE STORM, FOUGHT AGAINST THE BEAST OF EPHESIANS, BUT YOU KEPT THE FAITH. PRAISE THE LORD!

PRAYERS

HOW DO YOU STOP USING DRUGS? YOU MUST CONSTANTLY PRAY, AND ASK GOD TO TAKE THIS EVIL TASTE FOR DRUGS OUT OF YOUR MOUTH. THE LORD SAYS PRAY ALWAYS

WITHOUT CEASING AND ASK AND YOU SHALL RECEIVE. YET, YOU HAVE NOT BECAUSE YOU ASK NOT (Matthew 7:7), FOR YOU DO NOT KNOW GOD'S PURPOSE IN THIS LIFE FOR YOU NOR DO YOU KNOW WHAT A DAY WILL BRING (Proverbs 27:1). THUS, HOW DO YOU KNOW GOD DID NOT SEND YOU FORTH INTO THE WORLD OF DRUGS TO SAVE THOSE WHO ARE DYING AND ADDICTED TO DRUGS? IN YOUR ADDICTION, GOD SAW THE GOOD IN YOU. BUT YOU THEN BEING EVIL, STILL DO NOT KNOW YOU (Luke 11:13). YET, YOU ASK "WHY ME LORD" AND "WHAT MUST I DO" WHEN ALL THE TIME GOD IS TALKING TO YOU. YOU HAVE A GOOD HEART, BUT DRUGS REVEAL THE CONTENTS OF YOUR HEART. YET, "YOU ARE WHICHEVER YOU ARE." THUS, IF YOU ARE A EVIL, WICKED, AND NO GOOD PERSON THEN YOUR DRUG ADDICTION WILL REVEAL IT UNTO YOU. YOU CAN NOT FOOL YOU! HOW LONG DO YOU THINK YOU HAVE BEFORE THE DOG BITES? YOU HAVE JUST THAT MUCH TIME LEFT IN YOUR ADDICTION TO START DOING THE RIGHT THING. SURELY, GOD HAS MANIFESTED UNTO YOU THAT THE HOUNDS OF YOUR ADDICTION ARE HUNTING YOU AND THEY WILL NOT REST NOR BE CONTENT UNTIL THEY HAVE DEVOURED YOUR FRIGHTENED LITTLE SOUL IN HELL. BY THE GRACE OF GOD, YOU ESCAPED THROUGH THE GATES OF HELL DURING YOUR DRUG USAGE AND YOU GOT OUT WITH YOUR MIND WHEN YOU FOUND GOD IN YOU. YET, VERY FEW ADDICTS GET OUT WITH THEIR LIVES AND HARDLY ANYONE ESCAPES WITH THEIR MIND. BUT YOU FOUND THE GOD IN YOU AND MADE IT THROUGH. SATAN'S DEMONS WANTED TO BURN YOUR LITTLE FRIGHTENED SOUL IN HELL AND DECEIVE YOU UNTO DEATH, BUT GOD HAS ALWAYS BEEN THERE TO PROTECT YOU.

SATAN KNEW IT WAS YOU

SATAN KNEW YOU WERE HIGH, THE DAY YOU TRIPPED OVER A TOMBSTONE IN THE GRAVEYARD OF YOUR SUBCONSCIOUS MIND. HE KNEW AFTER YOUR FIRST HIT THAT ONE WOULDN'T BE ENOUGH AND A THOUSAND MORE WOULD NEVER BE ONE TOO MANY. HE KNEW YOU WOULD LOVE THE DRUGS JUST LIKE

ADAM AND EVE LOVED THE APPLE, BUT LIKE THE TWO OF THEM, YOU ONLY COMPLAINED WHEN YOU FOUND OUT THAT YOU WERE NAKED. YOU LOST YOUR TEETH, HEALTH, HOMES, CARS, BUILDINGS, BUSINESSES, JEWELRY, MONEY, WIFE, FAMILY, CHILDREN, FRIENDS, AND EVERYTHING YOU HAVE EVER OWNED. AT ONE TIME, YOU EVEN LOST YOURSELF. YOU LOST ALL THAT YOU ONCE HAD BECAUSE DRUGS STRIPPED YOU NAKED. YOU EITHER PUT ON THE PIPE, STUCK IN YOUR ARM, SNORTED UP YOUR NOSE OR, SWALLOWED IT WHOLE. WOE! SATAN IS STILL MAD IN HELL AT YOU BECAUSE YOU STOPPED USING DRUGS WHEN YOU FOUND THE GOD IN YOU. BUT YOU ARE STILL COMPLAINING TO GOD ABOUT THE THINGS YOU DID NOT GET AND DO NOT HAVE WHEN YOU SHOULD BE THANKFUL THAT GOD DIDN'T ALLOW SATAN TO GIVE YOU WHAT YOU TRUELY DESERVED. SATAN WANTED TO GIVE YOU MORE DRUGS, MORE DRUGS, AND MORE DRUGS UNTIL HE DECEIVED YOU UNTO DEATH. HE MADE SURE THAT IF YOU COULD NOT FIND DRUGS, DRUGS WOULD ALWAYS FIND YOU.

SATAN LITTLE IMPS

HAVE YOU EVER NOTICED THAT EVERY TIME YOU SAY YOU'RE GOING TO STOP USING DRUGS, THE DEVIL MAKES SURE THAT ONE OF HIS LITTLE IMPS COMES BY YOUR HOUSE TO GIVE YOU DRUGS? HAVE YOU EVER NOTICED THAT YOU GET MORE DRUGS WHEN YOU WANT TO STOP USING DRUGS? THAN YOU DOES WHILE YOU ARE CRAVING FOR DRUGS. WHY CAN'T YOU SEE THAT SATAN'S LITTLE IMPS USE DRUGS TO BECOME MORE OF THEMSELVES (devils)? WHENEVER YOU USE DRUGS, YOU BECOME SOMEONE ELSE. BUT WHO? THEY SAY THAT YOU ARE JUST PARANOID. THEY WALK THE DARKEST STREETS, THEY APPEAR OUT OF NOWHERE AT ANY TIME, AND THEY MOVE LIKE A SHADOW IN THE NIGHT, FOR THEY HAVE NO FEAR OF THE DARK BECAUSE THEIR DADDY IS THE PRINCE OF DARKNESS (Matthew 12:24). THEREFORE, THEY FEAR NOTHING OF THE NIGHT, BUT YOU. THEY KNOW THAT YOU'RE ANOINTED BY GOD WHILE YOU'RE IN THE SPIRITUAL WORLD

OF YOUR SUBCONSCIOUS MIND (high). GOD MAKES BAD THINGS HAPPEN TO THE LITTLE IMPS AROUND YOU.

SURROUNDED BY DEMONS

IN OTHER WORDS, WHILE YOU'RE IN YOUR SUBCONSCIOUS STATE, EVERYTHING AROUND YOU ARE SATANIC, AND ONE OF SATAN'S LITTLE IMPS. THEY ARE THERE TO DECEIVE YOU WHILE YOU ARE IN THIS DRUGGAFIED STATE OF MIND. YOU WILL SEE LITTLE IMPS GETTING SHOT, STABBED, AND BEATEN. YOU WILL SEE THEM ROBBING, STEALING, AND KILLING, BUT YOU'LL ALSO SEE THEM BEING PUNISHED BY THE WRATH OF GOD. FOR WHATEVER THEIR PUNISHMENT, YOU WILL KNOW, BUT NOT UNDERSTAND. ALTHOUGH, IN THE SPIRIT YOU'LL BE THANKFUL TO GOD THAT IT WASN'T YOU. YET, YOU'RE UNAWARE EVEN TO THIS DAY, THAT IT WAS ALL ABOUT YOU, ONLY YOU, AND NO ONE ELSE BUT YOU. YOU DON'T KNOW THE WORKS OF GOD, BUT YOU DO KNOW THAT WHATEVER IT WAS THAT HAPPENED, IT COULD NOT HAVE BEEN NOBODY BUT GOD. AMEN!

SATAN CHARGED HIS IMPS

SATAN CHARGED HIS LITTLE IMPS TO BEFRIEND YOU SO THAT HE CAN DECEIVE YOU UNTO DEATH, BUT GOD HAS ALWAYS BEEN THERE TO PROTECT YOU. WHEREAS, WHENEVER THEY SEE YOU, THEY SAY ONE TO ANOTHER "GET HIM, DADDY WANTS HIM! GET HIM, DADDY WANTS HIM! HURRY UP, AND LET'S GET HIM! DADDY WANTS HIM!" THUS, EARLY IN THE MORNING, THE LITTLE IMPS STARTED YOUR DAY OFF WITH ALCOHOL, FOR THEY KNOW ALCOHOL IS YOUR MAIN TRIGGER. AROUND NOONTIME, THEY ASK THEIR DADDY "IS HE READY FOR THAT HIT?" THEY GET NO REPLY, BUT THEY KNOW TO LEAVE YOU BEFORE YOU GET SPOOKED. HOWEVER, AT NOONTIME, SATAN SENDS SOME MORE OF HIS LITTLE MINIONS AND YOU'RE CONTINUOUSLY DRINKING AND GETTING DRUNK.

SATAN'S DAUGHTERS APPEARS

AGAIN, THEY ASK THEIR DADDY "IS HE READY FOR THAT BIG HIT?" THEY GET NO REPLY, BUT THEY ALSO KNOW TO LEAVE YOU BEFORE YOU GET SPOOKED. THEY KNOW THAT YOU'RE RELUCTANT TO HIT THE PIPE BECAUSE YOU ALREADY KNOW IT WILL BE A TRIP TO HELL. FOR YOU KNOW THE HOUNDS OF YOUR ADDICTION WILL BE COMING AND YOU CAN HEAR THEM BARKING BEFORE YOU TAKE YOUR FIRST HIT. YET, STAGGERING IN YOUR DRUNKEN STATE, BEFORE LONG SATAN'S DAUGHTERS APPEAR AND THERE'S NOT ONE YOU HAVEN'T SEDUCED ON DRUGS. THUS, BEHOLD! ONCE SUBDUED BY SATAN DAUGHTERS, THEY DISAPPEAR BACK INTO THE DARK JUST AS QUICKLY AS THEY SUDDENLY APPEARED INTO THE LIGHT. HOWEVER, UNLESS YOU CAN GIVE THEM MORE OF THEIR DADDY'S DRUGS. YOU WILL SPEND THE REST OF YOUR NIGHT SPRUNG, TWEEKING, TWERKING, PEEPING, GEEKING, MASTERBATING, AND LOSING YOUR MIND LOOKING FOR MORE MONEY TO BUY MORE DRUGS. WOE! THE LITTLE IMPS HAVE DECEIVED YOU. HAD YOU KNOWN THAT OUT OF 24 HOURS A DAY, GOD HAD ALLOWED SATAN ONE HOUR WITH YOU. FOR WOULD HAVE BEEN MORE WATCHFUL, BUT SATAN PICKS HIS HOUR AND HE KNOWS WHEN IT IS YOUR DRUNKEN TIME.

DESTRUCTION AT NOONDAY

THEREFORE, THE LAST STATE OF YOU IS FAR WORST THAN YOUR FIRST. FOR YOU WILL GO HOME LIKE A FLEA-BITTEN HOUND TO HIS MAT AND LAY THERE NAKED, LOOKING LIKE A BUCK-EYED FOOL STARING INTO TOTAL OBLIVION WITH NOTHING ELSE ON YOUR MIND EXCEPT ANOTHER PIECE OF DOPE. MY GOD, YOU DON'T SEE THE CHILDREN, HEAR THE WIFE, OR EVEN UNDERSTAND WHAT'S HAPPENING AROUND YOU. YOU ARE IN A MATRIX AND YOU ARE TRANSFIXED, DEMONIZED, AND AFRAID IN YOUR OWN HOUSE. WOE! YOU SENSE THE SAME TERROR BY NIGHT AS YOU SENSED YOUR DESTRUCTION AT NOONDAY (Psalm 91:5). THE DEAD ARE

AMONG YOU AND THE DEVIL IS TRYING TO LOCK YOU INTO YOUR SUBCONSCIOUS STATE OF MIND LEAVING YOU CONFUSED, TREMBLING, AND AFRAID. THERE YOU STAND TRYING TO SEE A THOUSAND MILES AWAY, BUT YOU CAN'T SEE UP CLOSE TO THE PROBLEMS YOU'RE CAUSING IN YOUR OWN HOME. MY LORD!

TROUBLED HOME INHERIT WIND

THE BIBLE SAYS, "HE WHO TROUBLES HIS OWN HOME SHALL INHERIT THE WIND." (Proverbs 11: 29) YET, DAY BY NIGHT, YOU SIT IN YOUR HOUSE SMOKING DRUGS LIKE A BROKEN CHIMNEY AND SHOOTING DOPE AS IF YOU HAVE LOST YOUR MIND. WHAT IS WRONG WITH YOU, DO YOU NOT SEE YOU? DO YOU NOT UNDERSTAND WHAT DRUGS MAKE YOU DO? THROUGHOUT YOUR NIGHTS OF CRAVING, YOU WILL PUSH YOUR PIPE, BURN YOUR FOIL, AND CLEAN YOUR NEEDLES. AFTER TAKING A GOOD BATHROOM HIT, YOU KEEP THE FAMILY UP ALL NIGHT. WOE! YOUR WIFE IS AFRAID OF YOU, THE CHILDREN ARE ASHAMED OF YOU, AND YOU DON'T KNOW WHAT TO DO ABOUT YOU. YOU CAN'T RUN FROM DEATH, BUT YOU ARE DIPPING, TIPPING, AND SLIPPING INTO THE FORBIDDEN WORLD OF YOUR SUBCONSCIOUS MIND. SATAN GIVES YOU ONE HOUR OF NAKED TORTURE, IMAGINARY SEXUAL TORMENTS, AND GREAT BALLS OF FEAR. WOE! THANKS BE TO GOD, YOU'RE A PRAYING MAN. AT THE BREAK OF DAWN, THE DEMONS FLEE FROM YOU AS YOU RETURN BACK INTO YOUR CONSCIOUS STATE OF MIND. YET, SATAN KNOWS IT'S JUST A MATTER OF A BIG BUMP, CRUMB, OR A GOOD PUSH, AND LIKE A DOG RETURNS TO HIS VOMIT, SO DOES MAN BACK TO HIS OWN WAYS (Proverbs 26:11). ONCE YOU TASTE TOMORROW'S DOPE, A TEAM OF WILD HORSES WILL NOT BE ABLE TO HOLD YOU BACK FROM ANOTHER HIT.

THE DEVIL HAVE YOU TRAPPED

WHAT ARE YOU GOING TO DO TO ESCAPE YOUR ADDICTION, SINCE YOU THINK YOU DON'T HAVE TO PRAY? ASK YOURSELF WHO ELSE CAN PROTECT YOU FROM THE DEVIL OTHER THAN GOD? ASK YOURSELF WHO ELSE CAN DELIVER YOU FROM DRUGS OTHER THAN GOD. ASK YOURSELF WHO ELSE CAN HELP YOU FIND THE GOD IN YOU, OTHER THAN YOU IN GOD. SURELY, NOT JUST YOU. WHAT CAN YOU DO? SATAN RUN FROM GOD TO YOU, AND YOU RUN FROM GOD TO WHO? THE DEVIL HAVE YOU TRAP, AND DRUGS ARE NO LONGER ENJOYABLE TO YOU. TODAY WHEN YOU USE DRUGS THE DEVIL TORMENTS YOU WITH EVEN GREATER FEAR. WOE! FOR DRUGS TRIPS YOU COMPLETELY OUT OF YOUR MIND. YOU GO CRAZY AFTER YOUR FIRST HIT. YOU FEEL LIKE SNAKES, SPIDERS, ANTS, BUGS OR SOMETHING CRAWLING ALL OVER YOUR BODY. OTHER TIMES, IT RUN YOU INTO A CLOSET, UNDER THE BED, OR IF NOT OUT OF THE HOUSE. WOE! FOR YOU KNOW HOW SCARED YOU GET WHEN YOU HIT THAT GOD FORSAKEN PIPE. YOU STAND THERE SHAKING IN YOUR BOOTS, WITH YOUR HANDS IN YOUR POCKETS, AND READY TO GO EVERY TIME YOU GET HIGH.

YOU CAN'T CON GOD

BUT THE LITTLE IMPS SAY YOU'RE JUST PARANOID. FOR YOU'RE DYING, AND HALF DEAD WHILE YOU LIVES. YOU ALREADY KNOW IF YOU KEEP USING DRUGS, DRUGS WILL BE THE DEATH OF YOU. DON'T YOU? YOU KNOW DRUGS MAKES YOU NERVOUS, FREAKY, HORNY, AND AFRAID, OH PATHETIC YOU! SATAN MAKES YOU DO ANYTHING FOR DRUGS, AND DRUGS DON'T LOVE YOU! BUT YOU KEEP HOLDING ON TO SOMETHING THAT'S TRYING TO DESTROY YOU. WHAT'S WRONG WITH YOU? DO YOU NOT SEE YOU? DO YOU NOT UNDERSTAND WHAT DRUGS MAKE YOU DO? THEN WHAT'S ABOUT YOUR ADDICTION YOU DON'T UNDERSTAND THAT'S TRUE? YET, TO LIVE IS TO UNDERSTAND THIS BOOK ABOUT YOU, AND DO EXACTLY WHAT GOD SAY YOU MUST DO. YOU

MUST GET DOWN ON YOUR KNEES AND PRAY EVERY NIGHT AND EVERY DAY. THERE'S NO IFS, ANDS OR BUTS ABOUT IT. THE CON STOP HERE! YOUR LIFE AT STAKE, AND YOU CAN'T CON GOD! YOU MUST PRAY, FAST, AND PRESS YOUR WAY THROUGH YOUR ADDICTION TO FIND THE GOD IN YOU. AT ONE TIME, GOD ALLOWED YOU TO USE DRUGS, AND HAVE YOURSELF A FREAKING GOOD TIME GETTING HIGH. BUT NOT ANYMORE! SATAN WICKED DOPE HAVE TURNED YOUR FREAKING GOOD TIMES INTO A DEADLY FEAR, AND YOUR GETTING HIGH INTO THE GRAVEYARD OF AN UNKNOWN DEATH. WOE! DO YOU HONESTLY THINK YOU CAN STOP USING DRUGS ON YOUR OWN, AND WITHOUT GOD?

YOU'RE DECEIVED

YOU ARE UNDOUBTLY DECEIVED BY THE DEMONS OF YOUR ADDICTION IF YOU TRULY BELIEVE THAT YOU COULD STOP USING DRUGS ON YOUR OWN AND WITHOUT GOD. HAVEN'T YOU LEARNED YET THAT SATAN SUPPLIES YOU WITH DRUGS TO POSSESS YOU? IN THE ARENA OF DRUGS, YOU ARE DUMB, NAÏVE, AND GULLIBLE ABOUT DOPE. WHAT DO YOU KNOW ABOUT DRUGS OTHER THAN HOW TO TOOT IT, SHOOT IT, BUT NOT BOOT IT? UNFORTUNATELY, IT MAKES NO DIFFERENCE WHAT YOU KNOW WHEN YOU STILL USE DRUGS! WHAT YOU DON'T KNOW IS THAT SATAN IS PLANNING ON STICKING A FORK IN YOU, FOR YOU ARE ALMOST DONE AND ANOTHER PIECE OF DOPE WILL SERVE YOU WELL. YOU ARE IN THE GRAVEYARD OF YOUR ADDICTION, BUT YOU THINK YOU CAN KEEP GETTING HIGH AND STAYING AHEAD OF THE GAME. THERE IS NOT A DEAD ADDICT YET WHO HAS NOT THOUGHT THIS WAY, NOR HAS THERE BEEN A LIVE ADDICT WHO HAS NOT HAD THOSE THOUGHTS. WHAT YOU DON'T KNOW, BLACK SHEEP, IS WHEN YOU USE DRUGS, YOU'RE PLAYING A GAME ONLY PLAYED BY THOSE WHO SEEK DEATH (Proverbs 21:6). THERE IS NO OTHER WAY THE GAME IS PLAYED. YOU HAVE AUTOMATICALLY BET YOUR LIFE BY BEING A PLAYER. SATAN WANTS YOUR SOUL (Luke 31:34) (1 Peter 5:8)!

DOMINION OVER ADDICTION

HOW DO YOU STOP USING DRUGS? ASK YOURSELF WHAT IN YOUR ADDICTIVE LIFE DID GOD NOT GIVE YOU DOMINION OVER? (Genesis 1:26) CERTAINLY NOT DRUGS. GOD GAVE YOU DOMINION OVER ALL THINGS AND YOUR ADDICTION ACCORDING TO GOD IS JUST ANOTHER THING. GOD GAVE YOU POWER OVER YOUR ADDICTION, NOT YOUR ADDICTION POWER OVER YOU. FOR YOU MUST BELEIVE IN THE POWER OF GOD VESTED WITHIN YOU, OTHERWISE, YOUR ADDICTION WILL BECOME YOU AND THE DEMON OF AN ADDICTION WILL MAKE YOU A DEVIL. YOU WILL NO LONGER BE YOU, BUT INSTEAD, THE EVIL DEMON WIITHIN YOU. GOD GAVE YOU DOMINION OVER DRUGS AND POWER OVER EVERY DEVIL IN HELL. THUS, DO YOU THINK SATAN'S DRUGS ARE STRONGER THAN THE GOD IN YOU? THE DEMON OF AN ADDICTION HAS DECEIVED YOU BECAUSE YOU THINK THE DEVIL'S DRUGS ARE STRONGER THAN THE GOD IN YOU. YOU SAY YOU LOVE THE WAY DRUGS MAKE YOU FEEL, BUT LOOK HOW SCARED YOU FEEL AFTER YOU FEEL WHAT YOU FEEL. KNOW YOU NOT FEAR COMES FROM SATAN (1 Peter 5: 8)? GOD DIDN'T GIVE YOU THE SPIRIT OF FEAR, BUT OF POWER, LOVE, AND OF A SOUND MIND (2 Timothy 1:7). WHAT IS WRONG WITH YOU? KNOW YOU NOT THAT WHEN YOU USE DRUGS, YOU ARE NOT YOU? THEN UNDERSTAND YOU! YOU THINK TOO POSITIVE ABOUT A DRUG THAT IS TOTALLY NEGATIVE TO YOU. YOU THINK TOO POSITIVE ABOUT A DRUG THAT IS BENEATH YOU AND YOU THINK TOO POSITIVE ABOUT A DRUG THAT'S GOING TO DESTROY YOU. THUS, ARE YOU SURE YOU KNOW WHEN YOU'RE NOT YOU? WHAT ABOUT RIGHT NOW, ARE YOU NOW YOU? WELL, WHAT ABOUT YOUR CHILDREN, ARE THEY NOT A PART OF YOUR ADDICTION? LISTEN YOU! THEY SUFFER THE SAME FATE OF YOUR ADDICTION AS YOU! OF COURSE, YOUR ADDICTIVE THOUGHTS OF YOUR HABITUAL NEGLECT HURTS, BUT WHAT ABOUT THEM? AND WHAT ABOUT YOUR FAMILY? SHOULD THEY SUFFER THE SAME ADDICTION AS YOU?

AS A MAN THINKETH SO IS HE.

UNDERSTAND YOU! THROUGH THE TRANSFORMATIONS OF YOUR MIND, GOD WILL DELIVER YOU (Romans 12:2). AS A MAN THINKETH IN HIS HEART, SO IS HE (Proverbs 23:7). SINCE YOU THINK YOU ARE ADDICTED TO DRUGS, THEN UNDOUBTELY YOU ARE ADDICTED TO DRUGS. SINCE YOU THINK YOU ARE A DRUG ADDICT, THEN UNDOUBTELY YOU ARE A DRUG ADDICT. SINCE YOU THINK YOU CAN NOT GET OFF DRUGS, THEN UNDOUBTELY YOU CAN NOT GET OFF DRUGS. IT IS YOUR SELF DEFEATING THOUGHTS THAT KEEP YOU ADDICTED TO DRUGS. HOW CAN GOD DELIVER YOU FROM DRUGS WHEN YOU THINK YOU ARE ADDICTED TO DRUGS? DIDN'T GOD JUST TELL YOU THAT YOU ARE NOT ADDICTED TO DRUGS UNLESS YOU THINK YOU'RE ADDICTED TO DRUGS? CHANGE YOUR THOUGHTS SO THAT GOD CAN DELIVER YOU FROM DRUGS. FOR YOU ARE NOT ADDICTED TO DRUGS AND YOU ARE NOT A DRUG ADDICT. YET, YOU ARE SO POSITIVE THAT YOU ARE ADDICTED TO SOMETHING THAT IS POSITIVELY EVIL. YOU SHOULD BE MORE POSITIVE THAT YOU ARE NOT ADDICTED TO DRUGS THAN YOU ARE ADDICTED TO DRUGS.

IN OTHER WORDS, QUIT THINKING YOU ARE ADDICTED TO DRUGS WHEN YOU ARE NOT ADDICTED TO DRUGS. QUIT THINKING YOU ARE A DRUG ADDICT WHEN YOU ARE NOT A DRUG ADDICT. QUIT THINKING THAT GOD WILL NOT DELIVER YOU FROM THE DEMON OF AN ADDICTION. THE DEVIL'S STRONGHOLD OF AN ADDICTION IS TO MAKE YOU THINK YOU ARE ADDICTED. YET, THERE IS A GOD IN YOU THAT CAN DO ALL THINGS THROUGH CHRIST WHICH STRENGHTENS YOU (Philippians 4:13). YOU MUST CALL OUT THOSE THINGS THAT ARE NOT AS THOUGH THEY WERE SO (Romans 4:17). YOU MUST SPEAK THINGS INTO EXISTENCE, SUCH AS TO YOUR DELIVERANCE, AND GOD WILL PROVIDE. (Proverbs 18:21) IT IS NOT SO MUCH AS WHAT YOU DO, AS IT IS THE GODLY THOUGHTS OF YOU.

CAST OLD YOU OUT

HOW YOU STOP USING DRUGS? YOU MUST CHANGE THE THINGS THAT CAUSED YOU TO BECOME ADDICTED TO DRUGS, INCLUDING YOUR THOUGHTS. IN OTHER WORDS, THE SAME OLD YOU HAS GOT TO GO. IT IS TIME TO CAST THE OLD MAN OUT (2 Corinthians 5:17). YOUR UNGODLY WAYS LED TO YOUR ADDICTION, AND THE SAME PEOPLE, PLACES, AND THINGS WILL KEEP YOU ADDICTED. THEREFORE, IT IS IMPERATIVE THAT YOU CHANGE YOUR WAYS COMPLETELY. STOP GOING TO THE SAME PLACES YOU USED TO GO. STOP BEING AROUND THE SAME MISFITS YOU USED TO BE AROUND AND LEARN TO SAY NO WHEN SATAN'S CHILDREN OFFER YOU DRUGS. YOU DON'T NEED DRUGS IN THE CONDITION YOU'RE IN. YOU NEED PRAYER. THE BIBLE SAYS, "THE EFFECTUAL FERVENT PRAYER OF A RIGHTEOUS MAN AVAILETH MUCH." (James 5:16). YOU NEED TO GET DOWN ON YOUR KNEES AND PRAY. DO NOT GET UP UNTIL YOU ARE SURE GOD HEARD YOU AND NOT UNTIL HE DOES. LISTEN YOU! DO YOU WANT TO LIVE? GOD SAYS, "CHOOSE YOU THIS DAY TO WHOM YOU SHALL FEAR." (Joshua 24:15) DO YOU FEAR GOD OR DO YOU FEAR THE DEVIL? DON'T BE AS HE WHOM GOD HAS TAKEN THE TASTE OF DRUGS OUT OF HIS MOUTH, BUT LETS SATAN PUT MANIPULATIVE THOUGHTS INTO HIS MIND.

WORKING IN THE DEVIL'S WORKSHOP

HE THINKS HE CAN SELL DRUGS AND GET THE MONEY BACK HE SPENT ON HIS ADDICTION. UNDERSTAND YOU! WHEN YOU SELL DRUGS YOU ARE WORKING IN THE DEVIL'S WORKSHOP. YOU MAY NOT BE AWARE OF THIS AS A DRUG DEALER, BUT THROUGH YOUR DRUG DEALING EFFORTS, SATAN WILL MAKE YOU BECOME ONE OF HIS LITTLE IMPS EVEN THOUGH YOU MAY NOT WANT TO BECOME ONE. YET, YOU WILL KNOW WHEN YOU BECOME ONE BECAUSE YOU WILL LIVE OUT THE TRUE NATURE OF THE DRUGS, FOR DRUGS ARE EVIL, WICKED, AND NO GOOD. ARE YOU EVIL, WICKED, AND NO GOOD? YOU ARE WHICHEVER YOU ARE. WHEN YOU SELL, DRUGS DO YOU KNOW WHO YOU ARE? HOW MANY PEOPLE HAVE YOU ROBBED FOR DRUGS?

HOW MUCH DOPE HAVE YOU SOLD FOR THE DEVIL? PLEASE DON'T SAY YOU HAVE KILLED SOMEBODY BECAUSE YOU OWE GOD YOUR LIFE. YOU ALLOWED DRUGS TO DARKEN YOUR HEART. AS SELF-RIGHTEOUS AS YOU WERE BORN, YOU ALLOWED DEATH TO WORK THROUGH YOUR MEMBERS. WOE! YET, GOD FORGIVES YOU, FOR SIN IS SIN, AND YOUR SIN IS NO GREATER THAN ANY OTHER SIN, EXCEPT BLASPHEME OF THE HOLY GHOST (Matthew 12: 31-32). THIS, YOU HAVE NOT DONE. GOD KNOWS WHEN YOU WERE SELLING DRUGS, YOU WERE UNAWARE THAT YOU WERE SELLING DEATH. WOE!

SATAN PLAY FOR SOULS.

YOU WERE SELLING DEATH AT ALL CAUSES AND YOUR ADDICTION TO SELLING DEATH WAS SIX TIMES MORE ADDICTIVE THAN AN ADDICT USING DRUGS. WOE! THE DRUGS YOU ARE SELLING ARE THE SUBTLE, EVIL, WICKED, SEDUCTIVE, AND DECEITFUL SPIRITS OF THE DEVIL. WOE! YOU ARE TRANSFORMING THE CONSCIOUS STATE OF THE CARNAL MIND INTO THE SUBCONSCIOUS MIND OF SPIRITUAL WARFARE. THUS, TO BE TORMENTED WITH FEAR, VEXED BY A SEDUCING SPIRIT, AND POSSESSED BY THE DEVIL. WOE! AS A WORKER OF SATAN, NOTHING GOOD WILL BECOME OF YOU. BUT YOU WOULD NOT KNOW THIS BECAUSE YOU HAVE ALWAYS BEEN A DRUG ADDICT. OR HAVE YOU? SATAN REWARDS DRUG DEALERS WITH PRETTY WOMEN, NICE CARS, FLASHY JEWELRY, AND DEATH. THE GLORY SATAN GIVES TO A DRUG DEALERS IS AN ILLUSION THAT WOULD DISSIPATE DURING THEIR DAY IN COURT. YET, SATAN PLAYS FOR SOULS, NOT LIVES AND HE PLAY FOR KEEPS. HE KNOWS YOU CAN LIVE EARTHLY WITH YOUR SOUL BUT WITHOUT YOUR SOUL, YOU CAN NOT LIVE ETERNALLY. YOU ARE JUST AS YOU ARE TODAY—ALIVE! BUT YET, NOT DEAD, FOR YOU HAVE NO DIRECTION IN LIFE AND NO PURPOSE FOR BEING HERE. YOU LIVE ONLY TO EXIST AND HAVE NO SENSE OF WORTH. WOE! SATAN DECAPITATES YOUR HEAD WITH EXTREME FEAR EVERY TIME HE DECEIVES YOU INTO USING DRUGS.

GOD CORRECT THE CHILD HE LOVE

BLACK SHEEP, GOD CORRECTS THE CHILD WITH WHOM HE LOVES (Proverbs 3:12), BUT PRIDE GOES BEFORE DESTRUCTION AND A HAUGHTY SPIRIT BEFORE A FALL (Proverbs 16:18). SATAN DECEIVES DRUG DEALERS WITH AN ILLUSION OF GETTING RICH, BUT AT THE END OF THE GAME THEREOF, ALL THEY FIND ARE THEIR OWN ADDICTIONS, DEATH, OR THE PENITENTIARY. WOE! NOBODY WINS WITH THE DEVIL, WHETHER YOU'RE A USER, A SELLER, OR AN ADVOCATE OF DRUGS. SATAN HAS SOLD THIS LIE FOR YEARS AND THERE IS NOT ONE OF THE THREE ABOVE WHO HAS NOT BEEN DECEIVED BY IT YET. THEY HAVE ALL BEEN DECEIVED, BUT THIS BOOK IS NOT ABOUT HOW YOU COULD START SELLING DRUGS AND BECOME YOUR OWN BEST CUSTOMER, BUT ABOUT HOW TO STOP USING DRUGS BY KNOWING YOU AS A CUSTOMER. YOU ARE A CUSTOMER TO SATAN'S LITTLE IMPS AND YOU ARE A GOOD CUSTOMER AT THAT. YOU HAVE PAWNED YOUR CAR, SPENT THE CHILDREN'S MONEY, AND NOW YOUR WIFE IS ON DOPE. WOE! AS A GOOD CUSTOMER, YOU TALK FOR DRUGS, RUN FOR DRUGS, AND STAY UP ALL NIGHT TRYING TO FIND DRUGS. YOU ARE SUCH A GOOD CUSTOMER THAT EVERY DRUG DEALER IN TOWN KNOWS YOU. YOU HAVE SMOKED WITH THE VERY BEST. NOW, AS A GOOD CUSTOMER, HOW MUCH MORE OF YOUR ADDICTION WOULD YOU LIKE TO CHARGE TO THE GAME? YOU CHARGE EVERYTHING YOU DO TO THE GAME, INCLUDING YOUR ADDICTION. TODAY, YOU KNOW EVERYTHING ABOUT THE DOPE GAME EXCEPT THAT YOU ARE PLAYING A DEAD HAND.

THE SERPENT!

HOW YOU STOP USING DRUGS? PONDER THE PATH OF LIFE AND REMEMBER ADAM. WHEN YOU BLAMED EVE, EVE BLAMED THE SERPENT, AND EVER SINCE THEN THE SNAKE HASN'T HAD A LEG TO STAND ON (Genesis 3: 13). YOU TOOK THE LEGS RIGHT OUT FROM UNDERNEATH HIM IN THE GARDEN OF EDEN

AND YOU CAN DO THE SAME IN YOUR EARTHLY TRANSGRESSIONS WITH DRUGS. THUS, "ON THY BELLY THOU SHALL GO, AND DUST SHALL THOU EAT ALL THE DAYS OF THY LIFE." (Genesis 3:14) WOE! WHAT A CURSE! EVERY TIME YOU HIT THE PIPE, THE CURSE OF GOD IS IN YOU. THE PIPE IS A SERPENT AND YOU ARE CURSED FOR USING IT. CALL IT A STEEL PIPE, GLASS PIPE, OR A PIPER'S PIPE, BUT A PIPE IS A SERPENT, AND THE SERPENT LIVES IN THE DEVIL'S HORN. YOU ARE CURSED FOR USING IT, BUT YOU COULD WEAN YOURSELF OFF THE PIPE JUST LIKE YOU WOULD WEAN A BABY OFF THE BOTTLE. HOWEVER, YOU CAN'T JUST CAP THE PIPE OFF WITH BRILLO, OTHERWISE, THE DOUBLE HEADED SNAKE WILL YOU HIT FROM BOTH END. WOE! YOU MUST WEAN YOURSELF OFF THE PIPE BY FINDING ANOTHER METHOD OF USING THE SAME DRUGS YOU ALREADY USE. REHAB CENTERS TEACH COMPLETE ABSTIENCE, BUT IF IT WAS THAT SIMPLE, YOU WOULD NOT NEED GOD. YOU HAVE BEEN TO REHAB CENTERS THREE TIMES, BUT YOU STILL USE DRUGS. WHY? THE CONCEPTS REHAB CENTERS TEACH ARE VERY GOOD CONCEPTS, BUT THEY ARE TAUGHT FROM AN EARTHLY PERSPECTIVE. THUS, THEY ARE INEFFECTIVE SPIRITUALLY IN CASTING OUT DEVILS. ONLY THE WORD OF GOD CASTS OUT DEVILS AND THERE'S NOT A REHAB CENTER IN THE UNITED STATES QUALIFIED TO PREACH IT (Mathew 12: 28)(Luke 11: 20).

METHODOLOGY AND PROCESS.

HOW DO YOU STOP USING DRUGS? UNDERSTAND YOU! NOT ONLY ARE YOU ADDICTED TO DRUGS, BUT YOU ARE ALSO ADDICTED TO THE "METHODOLOGY" AND "PROCESS" OF HOW YOU USE DRUGS. THE VERY THINGS YOU DO TO GET HIGH ARE THE SAME THINGS YOU HAVE ALWAYS DONE SINCE THE DAY OF YOUR ADDICTION. THUS, WOULD YOU LIKE A CIGARETTE BEFORE YOU GET STARTED ON YOUR METHOD? WELL, WHAT ABOUT A DRINK? OKAY, THEN GET NAKED AND COMFORTABLE BEFORE YOU TAKE A HIT! SO, YOU DON'T FEEL COMFORTABLE UNLESS YOU'RE AT YOUR OWN HOME WHEN YOU USE DRUGS?

HEY! WHERE'S THE LIGHTER? DON'T BURN UP MY PIPE! DON'T PUSH IT AND HURRY UP! I TOLD YOU NOT TO PUSH IT! DAMMIT! I MISSED MY HIT! ARE THESE WORDS FAMILIAR TO YOU DURING YOUR PROCESS? WHAT ABOUT YOUR METHOD? IF YOUR METHOD IS PUTTING DRUGS ON A PIPE THEN CHANGE THIS METHOD BY USING TOBACCO PRODUCTS. THE PIPE DEMON IN YOUR ADDICTION THAT LIKES HIS DRUGS ONLY ON THE PIPE WILL LEAVE THE ADDICTION BECAUSE YOU HAVE DENIED HIS ADDICTION. REMEMBER, YOUR ADDICTION IS NOT YOU, BUT A DRUG USING DEMON WITHIN YOU AND YOUR CRAVING FOR DRUGS IS THE DEMON OF AN ADDICTION.

THE WORD OF GOD CASTS OUT DEVILS

IN OTHER WORDS, YOUR DRUG ADDICTION IS A DRUG-USING DEMON WAITING TO BE CAST OUT BY THE WORD OF GOD, FOR ONLY THE WORD OF GOD CASTS OUT DEVILS AND YOU MUST USE GOD'S WORDS AS YOU USE DRUGS. GOD'S WORD IS AS A DOUBLE-EDGED SWORD. IT FIGHTS THE DEMONIC SPIRITS OF YOUR ADDICTION WHILE YOU ARE IN THE SPIRITUAL WORLD OF YOUR SUBCONSCIOUS MIND. HOWEVER, BE TRUE TO THE CAUSE WHEN YOU USE GOD'S WORDS. OTHERWISE, THE DOUBLE-EDGED SWORD WILL CUT YOUR HEAD OFF JUST AS SURE AS IT WILL THESE DEVILS. THUS, DO NOT PLAY WITH GOD, AND IN YOUR SINCERE EFFORTS TO WEAN YOURSELF OFF OF THE PIPE, GOD WILL ENABLE YOU TO ENDURE. A LOT OF PEOPLE WOULD ARGUE THAT YOU ARE STILL USING DRUGS, BUT THEY ARE AS UNAWARE AS YOU. YOU ARE NOT ADDICTED TO DRUGS, YOU RE ADDICTED TO THE METHODOLOGY AND PROCESS OF HOW YOU USE DRUGS.

TOBACCO DEMON ADDICTION

A TOBACCO DEMON WILL COME AFTER YOU STOP HITTING THE PIPE, BUT HIS POWERS ARE WEAK BECAUSE THE TOBACCO DEMON'S ADDICTION IS IN ITS EARLY STAGES, WHEREAS THE

PIPE DEMON HAS BEEN LONG IN HIS USAGE. YOU HAVE BEEN ON THE PIPE FOR THE LAST SIX TO TWELVE YEARS AND THE DEMONS OF YOUR ADDICTION HAVE GOT YOU THINKING ALL OF A SUDDEN; YOU CAN PUT THE PIPE DOWN. FOR ALL THESE YEARS YOU HAVE NOT BECAUSE YOU COULD NOT. IT IS NOT THAT SIMPLE AND YOU SHOULD KNOW THIS FOR YOURSELF, OTHERWISE, YOU WOULDN'T HAVE IT IN YOUR POCKET OR ALWAYS NEARBY WHEN YOU'RE READY TO USE IT. WOE! THE PIPE IS DELUSIONAL AND THE DEVIL'S HORN HAS DECEIVED YOU. YOU ARE UNAWARE THAT YOU ARE NOT ADDICTED TO DRUGS, BUT YOU ARE ADDICTED TO THE METHODOLOGY OF HOW YOU USE DRUGS. THE METHOD OF HOW YOU USE DRUGS IS THE PIPE, BUT YOU THINK BECAUSE YOU USE DRUGS, YOU'RE ADDICTED TO DRUGS, SO YOU WILL NEVER SEE YOUR TRUE ADDICTION TO THE PIPE. WOE!

PIPE DREAM

THE DEVIL HAS DECEIVED YOU AND BLINDED YOU TO THE FACT THAT YOU ARE NOT ADDICTED TO DRUGS, BUT TO THE PIPE. YET, YOU CARRY THE PIPE WHEREVER YOU GO AND YOU NEVER LEAVE HOME WITHOUT IT. HOWEVER, TO THINK THAT YOU CAN JUST UP AND QUIT HITTING THE PIPE WITHOUT TRYING EFFORTS, PRAYERS, AND WITHOUT GOD, IS A PIPE DREAM. YOU HAVE BEEN DECEIVED BY THE DEMONS OF AN ADDICTION, AND THAT IS WHY TO THIS DAY YOU STILL USE DRUGS. WHY? BECAUSE YOU STILL HIT THE PIPE AND YOU DO NOT SEE THE METHODOLOGY AS YOUR ADDICTOR. YOU ONLY SEE DRUGS AS YOUR ADDICTION! THUS, RIGHT NOW, YOU DO NOT KNOW WHETHER YOU'RE ADDICTED TO DRUGS OR THE PIPE. THE METHODOLOGY AND PROCESS OF HOW YOU USE DRUGS KEEPS YOU ADDICTED TO BOTH. YOU THINK YOU ARE ADDICTED TO JUST DRUGS, BUT YOU ARE NOT. YOU ARE ALSO ADDICTED TO THE PIPE AND IT IS THE DEMON THAT LIVES IN THE DEVIL'S HORN THAT KEEPS YOU ADDICTED TO DRUGS. DO YOU NOT SEE THE DIFFERENCES?

TWO ADDICTIONS

THERE IS A STRONG SIMILARITY BETWEEN THE TWO ADDICTIONS, BUT THERE IS A DIFFERENCE. THE PIPE IS A SLY DEVIL AND HE HIDES WITHIN YOUR ADDICTION TO AN ADDICTION. THE DEVIL WITHIN AN ADDICTION HIDES WITHIN AN ADDICTION TO AN ADDICTION. MY GOD! YOU WILL NEVER SEE YOUR ADDICTION TO THE PIPE BECAUSE IT IS OBVIOUS TO YOU AND EVERYONE WHO KNOWS YOU THAT YOU ARE ADDICTED TO DRUGS. THEREFORE, THE PIPE DEMON IN YOUR ADDICTION REMAINS UNNOTICED. WOE! THUS, YOU ARE LIKE A DOG CHASING HIS TAIL. HE WILL NEVER CATCH IT BUT, HE KEEPS RUNNING AROUND IN CIRCLE TRYING TO CATCH IT. THE DIFFERENCE IS YOU ARE NOT A DOG, THEREFORE, YOU MUST FIRST WEAN YOURSELF OFF THE PIPE BEFORE YOU CAN STOP USING DRUGS.

DEMON REBELLION

THE PIPE DEMON WITHIN YOUR ADDICTION WILL REBEL AGAINST THE TASTE OF THE DOPE BEING PUT ON TOBACCO BECAUSE IT IS NEW TO YOU AND TASTES HORRIBLE TO HIM. YOU DON'T KNOW THIS, BUT THE PIPE DEMON KNOWS YOU THINK YOU ARE ADDICTED TO JUST DRUGS, SO YOU WILL AGREE WITH THE DEVIL. WOE! THUS, BY CHANGING THE METHOD AND PROCESS OF HOW YOU USE DRUGS, THREE THINGS WILL HAPPEN BEFORE GOD DELIVERS YOU FROM THE DEMON OF A DRUG ADDICTION. YOU MUST UNDERSTAND THIS THREEFOLD DELIVERANCE. OTHERWISE, YOU MIGHT NOT MAKE IT THROUGH IT. IF YOU ARE ALREADY GOING THROUGH IT THEN LET THIS BE YOUR CONFIRMATION.

FIRST PHASE OF DELIVERANCE

FIRST, BY USING TOBACCO PRODUCTS RATHER THAN HITTING THE PIPE, YOUR CRAVING FOR DRUGS WILL ALMOST BE THE

SAME. BUT YET, IT WILL BE MORE TOLERABLE AND LESS DEAMNDING THAN HITTING THE DEVIL'S HORN. DRUG ADDICTS WHO SMOKE PRIMOS, TOOT POWDER, AND NEVER HIT THE PIPE MAINTAIN THEIR ADDICTIONS AND ARE ABLE TO STOP USING DRUGS MUCH FASTER THAN THOSE WHO HIT THE DEVIL'S HORN. THE PIPE IS HOLLOW AND YOU CAN NEVER FILL THE VOID OF YOUR HOLLOW DESIRES FOR MORE DRUGS. YOU WILL ACT DIFFERENTLY FROM THOSE WHO HIT THE PIPE, BUT WHEN YOU TOOT THE HORN, YOU WILL DANCE TO THE SERPENT IN THE FLUTE. ONCE SPRUNG, YOU WILL BECOME AS WORRISOME AS A GNAT, BOTHERSOME AS A FLY, AND ABOUT AS CRAZY AS A BESSIE BUG. THE PIPE DEMON WILL HAVE YOU DOING ALL KINDS OF WEIRD AND UNUSUAL THINGS, FOR YOU WILL BE CONSTANTLY MOVING, BEGGING, FIENDING WITH BUCKEYES, AND LOOKING FOR ANY KIND OF WAY TO GET MORE MONEY TO BUY MORE DRUGS. THEREFORE, BY CHANGING THE METHOD OF HOW YOU USE DRUGS, YOU WILL HAVE MORE CONTROL OVER YOU IN YOUR ADDICTION WHICH SHOULD BE YOUR MAIN OBJECTIVE.

SECOND PHASE OF DELIVERANCE

SECOND, YOU WILL REQUIRE LESS DRUGS THAN YOU DID BEFORE BECAUSE A LITTLE HIT NOW WILL SCARE THE LIVING HELL OUT OF YOU. THE TOBACCO DEMON WILL RELEASE IN YOU THE LEGION OF PIPE DEMONS AND THE VERY LEAST PIECE OF DOPE YOU HIT, WILL SCARE YOU INTO A FRIGHTENED TRANCE. THUS, BE STILL. GOD IS WITH YOU! THE DEMONIC SPIRIT IS AWARE THAT YOU ARE WEANING YOURSELF OFF DRUGS AND SATAN KNOWS YOU ARE TIRED OF USING DRUGS. THEREFORE, EVERY TIME YOU TAKE A HIT, WHETHER IT BE TOBACCO OR ON THE PIPE, YOU WILL THROW THE REST OF YOUR DRUGS AWAY OUT OF GODLY FEAR AND HUMAN VULNERABILITY. THESE DEVILS WILL HAVE YOU SO NERVOUS, FEARFUL, AND AFRAID, FOR ALL YOU'LL SENSE IS DEATH. WOE! BE STILL, GOD IS WITH YOU.

GREAT FEAR!

THE FEAR YOU WILL BE EXPERIENCING WOULD BE ENOUGH TO DRIVE YOU TOTALLY INSANE, IF NOT MAKE YOU FAINT. WOE! I AM TALKING GREAT, TREMBLING, FEAR OF WHICH YOU HAVE NEVER KNOWN BEFORE. FEAR SO UNIMAGINABLE, SO INTENSE, AND SO DEADLY YOU ARE SUBJECT TO JUMP UP, AND RUN FROM YOUR OWN SHADOW. MY LORD! THUS, BE STILL, GOD IS WITH YOU. YOU ARE UNDER A DEMONIC ATTACK AND EVERY DEVIL IN HELL IS WINKING AT YOU. THEY ARE LAUGHING AT YOU BECAUSE YOU ARE BEING TORMENTED BY SATAN AND YOU ARE AFRAID OF DYING. MY GOD! BUT, BE STILL. GOD IS WITH YOU. REFER TO THE SCRIPTURE OF ISAIAH. "NO WEAPON THAT IS FORMED AGAINST THEE SHALL PROSPER; AND EVERY TONGUE THAT SHALL RISE UP AGAINST THEE IN JUDGEMENT THOU SHALT CONDEMN. THIS IS THE HERITAGE OF THE SERVANTS OF THE LORD, AND THEIR RIGHTEOUSNESS IS OF ME, THUS, SAITH THE LORD." (Isaiah 54:17) THE WORD OF GOD SHALL PROTECT YOU IN YOUR EFFORTS TO WEAN YOURSELF OFF DRUGS, FOR GOD WILL KNOW IF YOU ARE SINCERE ABOUT WEANING YOURSELF OFF THE PIPE, CAN, FOIL, SOCKET RACHET, CAR ANTENNA, GLASS INSTRUMENTS OR ANY OTHER SERPENTS YOU HAVE USED TO SMOKE DRUGS. GOD ALREADY KNOWS THAT YOU HAVE SUFFERED ENOUGH IN YOUR DEMONIC ADDICTION TO WANT TO STOP USING DRUGS. HE KNOWS EXACTLY WHAT YOU NEED WHILE YOU SUFFER THE UNKNOWN FATE OF YOUR ADDICTION. YOU DO NOT KNOW WHAT YOU NEED, BUT GOD KNOWS AND YOU CAN NOT FIGHT THESE DEVILS BECAUSE THEY ARE NOT HUMANS. THEY ARE EVIL AND YOU ARE NOT EVIL. YOU ARE HUMAN.

THE DEVIL APPEARS

BE AWARE OF THE WEANING PROCESS. THE DEVIL HIMSELF WILL APPEAR. WHEN YOU HIT THE PIPE, THE DRUGS WILL COMPLETELY TAKE YOUR MIND. THE DEVIL WILL HAVE YOU DOING THINGS THAT ONLY MAKE SENSE TO YOU. YOU WILL

DIG A HOLE IN YOUR BACK YARD, TEAR UP THE FLOORS IN YOUR HOUSE, KNOCK HOLES IN YOUR WALL, OR RUN BUTT-NAKED SCARED INTO THE DARK, SCARY WOODS ALL BY YOURSELF. WOE! YOU WILL BE ON ONE AND WHILE IN THIS HALLUCINATORY STATE, THE PEOPLE AROUND YOU WILL THINK YOU ARE CRAZY. YOU WILL BE SO SCHIZY, PARANOID, AND AFRAID IT WILL BE AS IF IT IS YOUR LAST DAY ON EARTH. WOE! BE STILL, GOD IS WITH YOU. FOR NOT SERVING GOD OUT OF WISDOM, GOD IS GOING TO ALLOW SATAN TO TAKE YOU ON DOWN THROUGH THERE. AS FOR YOUR DRUG ADDICTION, GOD IS GOING TO CAST THOSE DRUG-USING DEMONS RIGHT UP OUT OF YOUR ADDICTION. AND YOU NEED TO START PRAYING RIGHT NOW THAT YOUR MIND DOES NOT GO ALONG WITH THESE DEVILS.

A LIVING DOG

YOU HAVE HEARD OF PEOPLE WHO HAVE LOST THEIR MIND TO DRUGS. YOU HAVE SEEN FIRST HAND WHAT DRUGS HAVE DONE TO YOU. NOW, KNOW THIS IF YOU WILL, ONLY THOSE WITH TRYING EFFORTS, SINCERE HEARTS, AND A MADE UP MIND SURVIVE THEIR DEMONIC ADDICTIONS, FOR A MADE UP MIND DOES NOT TURN BACK AND GOD DELIVERS OFF DRUGS THOSE WHO HUMBLE THEMSELVES BEFORE THE LORD. YOU ARE BLESSED TO BE READING THESE WORDS, FOR YOU KNOW YOURSELF YOU SHOULD HAVE BEEN DEAD. DON'T YOU? THANK GOD YOU ARE STILL ALIVE. A LIVING DOG IS BETTER THAN A DEAD LION (Ecclesiastes 9:4). HOPEFULLY, YOU HAVE NOT FORGOTTEN ABOUT YOUR ADDICTIVE FRIENDS WHO HAVE DIED IN THEIR ADDICTIONS, FOR WE PRAY THEY FOUND THE LORD BEFORE THEIR DEATH. YET, THIS BOOK IS ABOUT YOU,ONLY YOU, AND NO ONE ELSE BUT YOU. PRAISE THE LORD! YOU MADE IT THROUGH, FOR GOD DELIVERED YOU FROM WHAT YOU COULD NOT DO, AND THAT IS STOP USING DRUGS.

THIRD PHASE OF DELIVERANCE

DRUGS SIX TIMES DEADLIER

THIRD, DRUGS WILL BECOME SIX TIMES MORE DEADLY UPON YOUR EVERY USAGE, BUT BE NOT AFRAID. GOD IS IN CONTROL NOW AND THE LORD IS WITH YOU. YOU MUST SUBMIT YOURSELF TOTALLY UNTO THE WORKS OF THE LORD IF YOU WANT TO LIVE. YOU MUST DO THAT WHICH IS RIGHT IN GOD'S EYE, AND HE WILL DELIVER YOU. SATAN IS TRYING EVER SO HARD TO DESTROY YOU BECAUSE YOU HAVE ATTEMPTED TO STOP USING DRUGS. YOU DO NOT KNOW THIS, BUT THE DEVIL KNOWS BY YOU NOT HITTING THE PIPE, YOU WILL LEARN THAT YOU ARE NOT ADDICTED TO DRUGS. HE KNOWS BY YOU WEANING YOURSELF OFF THE PIPE, YOU WILL WEAN YOURSELF OFF THE DRUGS. HE KNOWS GOD WILL DELIVER YOU ONLY THROUGH YOUR TRYING EFFORTS. THEREFORE, HE MUST DESTROY YOU BEFORE YOU ESCAPE THROUGH THE DOOR OF YOUR ADDICTION. THE DOOR WAS CLOSED AND YOU WERE LOCKED WITHIN THE METHODOLOGY AND PROCESS OF HOW YOU USED DRUGS. SATAN HAS LOCKED YOUR MIND INTO THINKING YOU ARE ADDICTED TO DRUGS WHEN YOU ARE NOT. HE HAS LOCKED YOUR MIND INTO THINKING YOU ARE A DRUG ADDICT, WHEN YOU ARE NOT. HE HAS LOCKED YOUR MIND INTO THINKING YOU ARE HELPLESS TO DRUGS AND THAT YOU CAN NOT LIVE WITHOUT THE PIPE. HOWEVER, BY WEANING YOURSELF OFF THE PIPE, YOU HAVE UNLOCKED THE DOOR THAT MANY ADDICTS HAVE DIED TRYING TO FIND. THEY DID NOT KNOW HOW TO PIPE DOWN, BUT YOU DID. YOU KNOW THE METHODOLOGY AND PROCESS THAT KEEPS YOU ADDICTED TO DRUGS, FOR YOU NO LONGER PIPE FOR SATAN. THUS, YOU HAVE FOUNDED THE LORD. YOU BURIED YOUR HORN, NOT BURNED IT AND CROSSED BACK OVER TO GOD.

SATAN'S LAST CHANCE

SATAN CAN NOT ALLOW THIS TO HAPPEN AND THERE IS NO WAY IN HELL YOU SHOULD MISS YOUR NEXT HIT. THE HOUNDS OF YOUR ADDICTION ARE HUNTING YOU AND EVERY LITTLE IMP IN TOWN IS TRYING TO GET YOU HIGH AND GIVE YOU FREE DRUGS. THEY KNOW IF THEY CAN ENTICE YOU BY SHOWING YOU THE DRUGS, TALKING ABOUT DRUGS, OR USING DRUGS, YOUR ADDICTION WILL TRICK YOU INTO HITTING THE PIPE AND THE SPOOKY, SCARY HIGH WILL GIVE SATAN HIS LAST CHANCE TO TRY TO LOCK YOU INTO YOUR SUBCONSCIOUS STATE OF MIND. THEY KNOW WHEN SATAN LOCKS YOU INTO THE SPIRITUAL WORLD OF YOUR SUBCONSCIOUS MIND, THERE IS NO OTHER FACE YOU WILL SEE EXCEPT HIS. YOU WILL NEVER LIVE TO TELL WHO THE DEVIL IS. WOE! YOU WILL NOT ESCAPE DEATH BECAUSE EVERY MORBID THING AROUND YOU IS EITHER DYING OR ALREADY DEAD. WOE! MY GOD! BY KNOWING THE DEVIL IS IN YOU WHENEVER YOU USE DRUGS, YOU WILL DIE OVER AND OVER AGAIN IN YOUR CONSCIOUS MIND EVERY TIME YOU ESCAPE THE GRAVEYARD OF YOUR SUBCONSCIOUS DEATH. MY LORD! BECAUSE YOU ARE HELPLESS TO DRUGS, YOU WILL CRY "LORD SAVE ME!" AND HE WILL.

SATAN SHOWS HIS FACE

DURING THIS PHASE OF THE WEANING PROCESS, AFTER YOUR FIRST LITTLE HIT, THE SUDDEN FEAR OF THE DEVIL WILL COME UPON YOU QUICKLY AND YOUR MIND'S CONVICTIONS WILL HAUNT YOU LIKE A GHOST. WOE! YOU WILL NOT KNOW WHAT IS COMING AT YOU, WHO IS OUT TO GET YOU, OR WHERE THE DEVIL IS AT. YET, ALL THE TIME HE WILL BE IN YOU. WHILE BEING HIGH, YOU WILL THINK YOU SAW THE DEVIL, BUT BE STILL, GOD IS WITH YOU. YOU DID SEE THE DEVIL, BUT YOU DIDN'T HIS FACE. SATAN SHOWED HIS FACE WHEN YOU WERE IN THE SPIRITUAL WORLD OF YOUR SUBCONSCIOUS MIND, BUT IN YOUR DRUGAFIED STATE, YOU WERE TOO AFRAID TO LOOK AND TOO SCARED TO MOVE. MY

GOD! YOU WERE SO CAUGHT UP IN YOUR UNGODLY FEARS THAT ALL YOU COULD DO WAS PRAY. AMEN! HELP US LORD. SOMEHOW, PERHAPS BY SOMEONE PRAYING FOR YOU, YOUR SPIRIT SUBCONSCIOUSLY KNEW IT WAS THE DEVIL AND YOU ESCAPED THAT HORRIBLE, UNBELIEVABLE, FRIGHTFUL MOMENT OF YOUR PAST ORDEAL WITH DEATH BY THE GRACE OF GOD. FOR AS AFRAID AS YOU WERE, YET IT WAS YOUR FEAR THAT KEPT YOU ALIVE.

GOD SEND EVIL SPIRIT TO FIND YOU

MY GOD! THANK JESUS FOR THY DELIVERANCE, FOR ONLY YOU KNOW OF THE EVENT THAT YOU WENT THROUGH. BUT WITNESS THIS FOR YOURSELF; THAT IS IF YOUR MEMORIES STILL SERVE YOU CORRECTLY. DO YOU REMEMBER IN YOUR DRUGAFIED STATE THAT THERE WAS A TIME IN YOUR ADDICTION THAT WHATEVER WAS THERE, WAS NOT THERE. YOU SAW, BUT DID NOT SEE. YET, YOU KNOW YOU SAW, BUT WERE NOT SURE. WOE! IT WAS THE DEVIL, BUT YOU DID NOT SEE HIS FACE. SATAN HAS BEEN THERE ALL THE TIME WAITING ON YOU IN YOUR ADDICTION, BUT SO HAS GOD. GOD HAS ALWAYS BEEN THERE TO PROTECT YOU (Psalm 91:1-16). BUT, UNDERSTAND YOU! GOD WILL ALSO SEND AN EVIL SPIRIT TO YOU TO HELP YOU FIND YOU. WHAT? YOU DON'T THINK GOD WILL SEND AN EVIL SPIRIT TO YOU (1 Samuel 16:14-16)? HE IS GOD ALL BY HIMSELF, WHO CAN INSTRUCT HIM? NOT YOU!

PRAY, PRAY, AND PRAY

WHILE WEANING YOURSELF OFF DRUGS, YOU WILL HATE YOURSELF AND YOUR USAGE EVERY TIME THE DEVIL DECEIVES YOU INTO USING DRUGS; THE DRUGS YOU ONCE LOVED, WORKED FOR, ROBBED FOR, STOLE FOR, LIED FOR, AND ALMOST DIED FOR. YOU WILL HATE SATAN AFTER EACH OF YOUR FRIGHTENED USAGES. Matthew 6:24) YOU WILL PRAY DAY AND NIGHT AND NIGHT AND DAY THAT GOD DELIVERS

YOU EVERY TIME YOU ENTER INTO THE SPIRITUAL WORLD OF YOUR SUBCONSCIOUS MIND, FOR YOU WILL PRAY, PRAY, AND PRAY. GOD WILL DELIVER YOU THROUGH YOUR CONSTANT PRAYERS BECAUSE YOUR PRAYERS WERE ALL GOD NEEDED FROM YOU. "FOR IT IS WRITTEN, AS I LIVE, SAITH THE LORD, EVERY KNEE SHALL BOW TO ME, AND EVERY TONGUE SHALL CONFESS TO GOD" (Romans 14:11). YOU HAVE STARTED DOING EXACTLY WHAT GOD HAS ALWAYS WANTED YOU TO DO. YES LORD! YOU WILL CALL ON HIM AND HE WILL DELIVER YOU. GOD WILL BRING YOU THROUGH YOUR TRYING EFFORTS AND DELIVER YOU FROM THE DEMON OF YOUR DEMONIC ADDICTION (Luke 10:19).

A LOST SOUL

THERE IS NOTHING WORSE IN HELL THAN A LOST SOUL FOR THE DEVIL. ALL THE PAIN, FEAR, SORROW, SLEEPLESS NIGHTS, AND LONG SUFFERING SATAN PUT YOU THROUGH WERE MEANT FOR YOUR BAD. GOD TURNED IT ALL INTO YOUR GOOD (Genesis 50:20) (Ephesians 1:13, 14). BY THE GRACE OF GOD YOU HAVE WEANED YOURSELF OFF DRUGS AND TODAY YOU ARE A WALKING EPISTLE AND A LIVING TESTAMENT THAT GOD IS GOOD. YOU SPEAK GODLY, LIVE GODLY, AND TRY TO BE GODLY IN ALL YOUR WAYS. YOU HAVE SUBMITTED YOURSELF TOTALLY UNTO THE WORKS OF THE LORD AND GOD HAS RESTORED THAT WHICH SATAN HAS TAKEN FROM YOU. PRAISE HIS NAME! YOU HAVE FOUND SOMETHING THAT VERY FEW ADDICTS IN A LIFETIME EVER FIND. YOU FOUND YOU AND YOU MADE IT THROUGH YOUR ADDICTION. GOD HAS GIVEN BACK TO YOU YOUR MIND, MORE SUBSTANCE, AND ONCE AGAIN THE ABILITY TO BE A GREAT BEING. HALLELUJAH! FOR YOUR DRUG ADDICTION HAS STRIPPED YOU OF YOUR FALSE PRIDE AND GOD HAS OPENED YOUR EYES TO ANOTHER YOU, A WONDERFUL YOU. THUS, THE REAL YOU! FOR YOU NOW SEE THE ERROR OF YOUR WAYS WHICH WERE ALL HEADED TOWARDS THE FIRE AND BRIMSTONE OF HELL. THANK YOU JESUS (Revelation 19: 20)!

YOU WENT THROUGH HELL

SATAN PUT YOU THROUGH HELL DURING YOUR USAGE OF DRUGS, BUT YOU GOT OUT WITH YOUR MIND WHEN YOU FOUND GOD IN YOU. YOU WERE DELIVERED BY YOUR CONSTANT PRAYERS, TRYING EFFORTS, AND THE WEANING PROCESS. YOUR OBEDIENCE TO GOD'S WORDS AND THE SELF RIGHTEOUSNESS OF YOU DELIVERED YOU FROM THE DEMONS OF YOUR ADDICTION. YET, YOU DID NOT DELIVER YOU BY DOING WHAT YOU WANTED TO DO, BUT BY YOU DOING WHAT GOD HAS INSTRUCTED YOU TO DO. YOUR DELIVERANCE ALONE IS A BLESSING WITHIN ITSELF BECAUSE BY YOU DOING WHAT GOD HAS INSTRUCTED YOU TO DO. HIS WORDS HELP YOU FIND THE GOD IN YOU, BUT IF YOU DO NOT DO WHAT GOD SAYS DO, THEN YOU WILL NEVER FIND GOD IN YOU. THEREFORE, LET US GIVE THANKS TO THE ALMIGHTY GOD THAT BE IN YOU, OTHERWISE, YOU WILL STILL BE USING DRUGS NOT KNOWING WHAT TO DO. NO THANKS TO YOU THAT YOU MADE IT THROUGH, BUT ALL THANKS BE TO THE GOD IN YOU. YOU ARE TALKING TO ANOTHER YOU, WHO AS YOU, HAS DONE AS YOU DO, BUT HAS ALSO MADE IT THROUGH BY THE SAME GOD IN YOU. IT IS A CRYING SHAME FOR THOSE WHO DID NOT MAKE IT THROUGH, BUT THEY HAD THEIR CHANCE TO SERVE THE SAME GOD AS YOU. IT IS UP TO YOU TO DO WHAT GOD SAYS TO DO,OTHERWISE, YOU WILL NEVER FIND THE GOD IN YOU. YES, IT IS A CRYING SHAME FOR THOSE WHO DID NOT MAKE IT THROUGH, BUT GOD GAVE THEM THE SAME CHANCE THAT HE IS GIVING YOU, FOR IT IS UP TO YOU TO DO WHAT GOD SAYS TO DO. IF NOT, THE ANGEL DEATH WILL ALSO COME FOR YOU, YOU ARE WHICHEVER YOU ARE. BUT WHOEVER YOU ARE, YOU NEED GOD. YOU WILL NEVER MAKE IT THROUGH YOUR ADDICTION WITHOUT GOD AND YOU WILL NEVER BE DELIVERED FROM AN ADDICTION WITHOUT GOD, FOR YOUR HAPPINESS HAS GOD HIDDEN WITHIN YOUR ADDICTION ,TO AN ADDICTION, AS HE HAS IN ALL ADDICTIONS. THUS, UNDERSTAND YOU! DO NOT HIT THAT GOD FORSAKEN PIPE REGARDLESS OF WHAT AND YOUR LIFE WILL IMMEDIATELY CHANGE BECAUSE YOU WILL BE SO HAPPY YOU HAVE STOPPED USING DRUGS. (Psalm 1: 1-6) (Luke 6: 43-49)

THE PIPE ADDICTED YOU

HOW TO STOP USING DRUGS COME FROM KNOWING THAT IT WAS THE PIPE THAT ADDICTED YOU TO DRUGS. THEREFORE, YOU MUST UNDERSTAND IT IS THE PIPE THAT KEEPS YOU ADDICTED TO DRUGS. YOUR ADDICTION IS JUST THAT SIMPLE. HOW SIMPLE IT IS TO STOP USING DRUGS BY NOT HITTING THE PIPE. AS COMPLICATED AS AN ADDICTION MAY APPEAR TO BE, IT IS THE SIMPLICITY OF THE ADDICTION THAT YOU DO NOT SEE. THIS IS ALL TOO SIMPLE, BUT IT IS A COMPLICATED THING TO THOSE WHO HAVE BEEN PIPE-BITTEN. BLACK SHEEP, IF YOU WANT TO LIVE, YOU MUST FIRST WEAN YOURSELF OFF THE PIPE OR DIE IN YOUR DEMONIC ADDICTION. THINK ABOUT THIS. WHAT DID YOU DO TO GET HOOKED ON DRUGS? HOW DID YOU GET HOOKED ON DRUGS? WHO HOOKED YOU ON DRUGS? WHERE DID YOU GET HOOKED ON DRUGS AND WHY DID YOU GET HOOKED ON DRUGS? THE WHO, WHAT, WHEN, WHERE, AND WHY IS NOT IMPORTANT. "HOW" IS THE FACTOR. YOU BECAME ADDICTED TO DRUGS, HOW? BY HITTING THE PIPE! AND BY THE PIPE, YOU STAY ADDICTED TO WHAT? DRUGS! YOU ARE TALKING TO ANOTHER YOU AND NOT YOUR PIPE. YOUR PIPE WILL TALK TO YOU AND YOU WILL TALK BACK TO YOUR PIPE. YOU HAVE CALLED THE PIPE YOUR BROTHER, UNCLE, AND FRIEND. SOME OF YOU HAVE EVEN CALLED IT YOUR GOD. WOE!

HOW HARD THE PIPE HIT!

REHAB CENTERS WOULD ARGUE THAT YOU ARE TRADING ONE ADDICTION FOR ANOTHER, BUT THESE CENTERS DO NOT KNOW HOW HARD THE DEVIL'S HORN HITS! ONLY YOU KNOW THE PIPE IS DIABOLICAL AND IT IS THE DEVIL TO PUT DOWN. ONLY YOU KNOW HOW FEARFUL YOU BECOME WHEN YOU HIT THAT GOD-FORSAKEN THING, AND HOW HORNY, AND DRY YOUR MOUTH GETS. YET, YOU STAND THERE IN COMPLETE FEAR WITH A HARD FACE STARING WIDE-EYED INTO A MOUTH FULL OF NAKEDNESS. ONLY YOU KNOW THEY SHOULD BE

QUIET WHEN YOU TAKE A HIT. THEIR MOVEMENTS, NOISE, AND TALK GET ON YOUR NERVES. THE DRUGS HAVE YOU TRIPPING; YOU ARE HEARING THING ,AND NOW YOU ARE SCARED. WOE! ONLY YOU KNOW WHEN YOU ARE SPRUNG; YOUR HEART IS BEATING FASTER, AND YOU ARE RUNNING OUT OF BREATH. YOU ARE IN THE REALM OF YOUR SUBCONSCIOUS MIND, AND THERE SEEMS TO BE NO WAY OUT. SATAN IS TRYING TO LOCK YOU INTO THIS SCARY STATE OF YOUR

SUBCONSCIOUS MIND.

WITHIN YOURSELF IS A SILENT CRY FOR HELP, BUT TO WHO? YOU DO NOT PRAY, YOU DO NOT WORSHIP GOD, AND YOU DO NOT FEAR THE LORD. MY GOD! THE DEVIL HAS YOU TRAPPED, AND YOU ARE LOST IN THE GRAVEYARD OF YOUR SUBCONSCIOUS MIND. NOW YOU DO NOT KNOW WHETHER TO RUN OR STAY. THUS, YOU ARE TOO AFRAID, FROZEN, AND SCARED TO MOVE. WOE! ONLY YOU KNOW THAT YOU ARE TWEEKING, FIENDING, SCARED, TREMBLING, NERVOUS, SHAKING, AND RUNNING FROM THE INEVITABLE. EVERY TIME YOU HIT THAT GOD-FORSAKEN PIPE. ONLY YOU KNOW HOW YOU HAVE CONNED FOR DOPE, LIED FOR DOPE, BEGGED FOR DOPE, STOLEN DOPE, ROBBED FOR DOPE, AND EVEN SHOT SOMEBODY FOR SOME DOPE JUST TO PUT ON THAT GOD FORSAKEN PIPE. ONLY YOU KNOW, BUT NOW, ARE YOU NOT CONVINCED? NOT EVEN BY WHAT YOU KNOW? GOD IS GIVING YOU 90 DEGREE KNOWLEDGE OF YOUR SINFUL DRUG ADDICTION AND IF YOU DON'T WEAN YOUSELF OFF DRUGS BY NOT HITTING THAT GODFORSAKEN PIPE. THE DEMON OF YOUR ADDICTION WILL DESTROY YOU (1 Peter 5: 8). THUS, DO YOU NOT HEAR YOU? ANY OTHER METHOD YOU MAY CHOOSE TO USE OTHER THAN THROUGH YOUR VEINS OR UP YOUR NOSE IS SUFFICIENT UNTO THE WEANING PROCESS. AS LONG AS IT HELPS YOU STOP HITTING THAT GOD -FORSAKEN PIPE!

SURPREME WARNING FROM GOD

IF YOU KEEP HITTING THE PIPE THEN KNOW THIS, IF YOU WILL. YOU ARE FREAKING YOU OUT OF YOUR MIND! EVERY TIME YOU HIT THAT GOD-FORSAKEN THING AND YOU HAVE RUN OUT OF TIME IN YOUR ADDICTION, DEATH IS UPON YOU, AND THE HOUNDS OF HELL HAVE CAUGHT UP WITH YOU. YOU MUST SEEK GOD'S DELIVERANCE FROM THE DEMON OF THIS ADDICTION. OTHERWISE, THE DEVIL'S DOGS OF A DRUG ADDICTION WILL EAT YOUR FLESH. YOUR PIPE HIGH IS OVER AND GOD IS GIVING YOU A SURPREME WARNING THIS DAY (John 10: 27). THERE SHALL BE NO OTHER WARNING GIVEN UNTO YOU EXCEPT DEATH! THUS, DO YOU WANT TO LIVE OR DO YOU WANT TO DIE? IF YOU WANT TO LIVE YOU HAVE NO OTHER CHOICE IN THIS MATTER, BUT TO STOP HITTING THAT GOD FORSAKEN PIPE. GOD HAS MANIFESTED UNTO YOU THE SERPENT IS IN THE DEVIL'S HORN. YOU MUST PRAY, FAST, AND ASK GOD TO GIVE YOU STRENGTH. YOU ARE HELPLESS TO DRUGS AS LONG AS YOU HIT THAT GOD FORSAKEN PIPE (Hebrews 3: 15), BUT IF YOU TRY TO PUT THE PIPE DOWN, GOD WILL ENABLE YOU TO WEAN YOURSELF OFF DRUGS. YOU ARE A CHILD IN GOD'S EYES. LIKE A BABY, YOU GOT TO CRAWL YOUR WAY OFF DRUGS THROUGH YOUR PRAYERS. PACIFY YOUR WAY OFF THE PIPE BY CHANGING YOUR METHOD AND STAND ON YOUR FEET AS A MAN. HAVE FAITH THAT GOD WILL DELIVER YOU. GOD WILL DELIVER YOU THROUGH YOUR TRYING EFFORTS AND GOOD WORKS (Proverbs 16:7)(Psalms 34:14). IF YOUR WORKS CONTINUE TO BE EVIL AND YOU REFUSE GOD'S INSTRUCTIONS YOU'LL BE EATEN ALIVE BY THE RAW DOGS OF YOUR ADDICTION.

THIS BOOK IS ABOUT YOU

A LOT OF PEOPLE THINK YOU CAN QUIT COLD TURKEY AND WITHOUT THE WEANING PROCESS, BUT THEY ARE NOT YOU! THIS BOOK IS ABOUT YOU, ONLY YOU, AND NO ONE ELSE BUT YOU! YOU DON'T HAVE TO BE TOLD THAT YOU'RE IN OVER

*YOUR HEAD. YOU KNOW THIS FOR YOURSELF, THAT YOU'RE IN
THE GRAVEYARD OF YOUR ADDICTION, AND YOU ALONE WILL
DIE. NOT THEM! FOR YOU ALREADY KNOW IF YOU DON'T GIVE
UP THAT GOD FORSAKEN PIPE, THE DEMONS OF YOUR
ADDICTION ARE GOING TO DESTROY YOU. THIS YOU MUST
KNOW, THAT THOSE WHO TOOT THEIR HORNS BECOME
SUDDENLY AFRAID OF SOMETHING, BUT NOW YOU KNOW
EXACTLY WHAT IT IS. THE DEVIL! HOWEVER, A PIPE DEMON
WILL LEAVE YOU ONLY WHEN HE FINDS OUT THAT HE'S NOT
GETTING ANY MORE DRUGS. JUST LIKE YOU WOULD AT A DRUG
DEALER'S HOUSE WHEN YOU KNOW FOR SURE HE HAS GIVEN
YOU YOUR LAST HIT. YOU CAN BEG, KEEP COMING BACK TO
THE DEALER'S DOOR, OR GET KNOCKED UPSIDE THE HEAD
BEFORE HE HAS TO CONVINCE YOU THAT YOU'RE NOT GETTING
ANY MORE DRUGS. ONLY THEN, WILL YOU LEAVE THE SAME AS
THE PIPE DEMON—BECAUSE THEY ARE MANY. YOUR LONG
USAGE OF DRUGS HAS ALLOWED THE PIPE DEMON TO FORM A
LEGION AND EVERY TIME YOU HIT THE PIPE, YOU WILL HAVE A
BUNCH OF DEVILS IN YOUR HEAD. WOE! YOU BECOME CRAZY,
SCARED, AND STUPID WHEN YOU HIT THAT THING!*

BIND THE PIPE DEMON

*THEREFORE, YOU MUST BIND THE PIPE DEMONS BY THE
BLOOD OF THE CROSS IN THE NAME OF OUR LORD AND SAVIOR
JESUS CHRIST (Hebrews 9: 22)(1 John 1:7)(1 Peter 1-2). GOD
WILL FIGHT YOUR BATTLE AS YOU REBUKE SATAN IN CHRIST'S
NAME. THE DEVIL WILL FLEE FROM YOU IF GOD'S WORDS BE IN
YOU. YOU MUST USE GOD WORDS EVEN MORESO WHEN YOU
ARE GETTING HIGH. YES! ESPECIALLY WHEN YOU ARE USING
DRUGS BECAUSE THE WORD OF GOD WILL PROTECT YOU FROM
THE DEVIL WHILE YOU'RE IN THE SPIRITUAL WORLD OF YOUR
SUBCONSCIOUS MIND. OTHERWISE, SATAN WILL TRY TO LOCK
YOU INTO THAT SCARY STATE OF MIND UNTIL YOU ARE DEAD.
WILL YOU NOT LISTEN TO ANOTHER YOU, WHO AS YOU, DONE
AS YOU DO? YET, MADE IT THROUGH BY THE SAME GOD IN
YOU. FOR THIS IS WHAT YOU MUST DO AND THE DEVIL WILL*

FLEE FROM YOU. DO NOT HIT THAT PIPE REGARDLESS OF WHAT FROM THIS DAY FORTH AND YOUR ADDICTION WILL FLEE FROM YOU JUST LIKE THE DEVIL (James 4: 7).

MYSTERY OF AN ADDICTION

HOW DO YOU STOP USING DRUGS? UNDERSTAND YOU! THERE IS A MYSTERY TO AN ADDICTION. MANY ADDICTS HAVE DIED TRYING TO OBTAIN KNOWLEDGE OF THEIR ADDICTIONS. THEY DIED NOT KNOWING HOW TO STOP USING DRUGS. THEY KEPT USING DRUGS, AND USING DRUGS. THE DEVIL GAVE THEM MORE DRUGS. THEY DID NOT SEE THE DEMON HIDING WITHIN THEIR ADDICTIONS, THEY ONLY SAW THE DRUGS, AND THE DEVIL DECEIVED THEM UNTO THEIR DEATH. SO, THE MYSTERY OF A DRUG ADDICTION IS NOT THAT YOU ARE ADDICTED TO DRUGS, BUT YOU ARE TRAPPED BY THE DEMON OF A DRUG ADDICTION. THERE IS A DEMON THAT LIVES IN A DRUG ADDICTION AND THIS DEMON LOCKS YOU INTO THIS ADDICTION. YET, YOU WILL THINK IT IS YOUR ADDICTION RATHER THAN THE DEMON SATAN HAS ASSIGNED TO A DRUG ADDICTION. THAT IS WHY A DRUG ADDICTION IS THE WORST ADDICTION SATAN HAS USED AGAINST GOD, SOCIETY, AND YOU, FOR IT IS A DEMONIC ADDICTION WITH DEVILISH CRAVINGS AND DEADLY CONSEQUENCES.

HELD A PRISONER OF AN ADDICTION

IN OTHER WORDS, YOU ARE BEING HELD AS A PRISONER OF THIS ADDICTION AGAINST YOUR OWN WILL. MY LORD, YOU ARE TRAPPED BY THE DEMON OF THIS ADDICTION AND YOU CAN'T STOP USING DRUGS ON YOUR OWN BECAUSE IT IS EVIL. FOR YOU DID NOT CREAT EVIL, AND REGARDLESS OF HOW HARD YOU WILL TRY TO STOP USING DRUGS IT'S IMPOSSIBLE WITHOUT GOD. ONLY GOD CAN DELIVER YOU FROM THE EVIL OF THIS ADDICTION AND WITHOUT GOD'S DELIVERANCE FROM THE DEMON OF A DRUG ADDICTION, THE DEVIL WILL

*DESTROY YOU. ARE YOU LISTENING TO YOU? THEREFORE,
PRAY WHOLE-HEARTEDLY TO GOD THAT HE DELIVERS YOU
FROM THE DEMON OF A DRUG ADDICTION, OTHERWISE, THIS
DEMON WILL KEEP YOU ADDICTED UNTO DEATH. WOE! YOU
CAN WEAN YOURSELF OFF THE DEVIL'S HORN BY CHANGING
THE METHOD, BUT YOU HAVE TO PRAY, AND USE GOD'S
WORDS TO BE DELIVERED FROM THE DEMON OF A DRUG
ADDICTION. THE WORD OF GOD SPOKEN IN DUE SEASON WILL
CAST THE DEMON OUT OF A DRUG ADDICTION AND DELIVER
YOU FROM DRUGS.*

YOUR HIGH, THE DEMON

*HOW DO YOU STOP USING DRUGS? YOU MUST USE GOD'S
WORDS TO CAST THE DEMON OUT OF DRUGS! UNDERSTAND
YOU! THE DEMON OF A DRUG ADDICTION WILL ONLY APPEAR
IN THE ADDICTION WHEN YOU ARE USING DRUGS. IN OTHER
WORDS, WHEN YOU ARE GETTING HIGH. THAT IS BECAUSE
YOUR "HIGH" IS THE DEMON OF A DRUG ADDICTION. BEING
YOUR ADDICTION, HE KNOWS IT BETTER THAN YOU KNOW
DRUGS, FOR HE KNOWS ONCE A PLANT HAS BEEN DEMONIZED
BY MAN, IT IS DEMONIC. THUS, IT IS NO LONGER OF GOD, BUT
YOU DO NOT KNOW WHEN YOU USE DRUGS, YOU ARE GETTING
HIGH WITH THE DEVIL. WOE! THE PLANT BELONGS TO SATAN
AND THAT'S HOW HE DECEIVES YOU. RIGHT NOW, AT THIS
VERY MOMENT, THE DEMON HAS TOTALLY CONVINCED YOU
THAT YOU ARE A DRUG ADDICT. THIS DEMON HAS YOU
THINKING THAT YOU ARE ADDICTED TO DRUGS AND THAT IS
ABOUT AS GOOD AS IT GETS WHEN IT COMES TO
DEMONOLOGY. WHEREFORE, HOW CAN YOU CAST THE DEMON
OUT OF A DRUG ADDICTION? IT IS GOOD YOU ASKED YOURSELF
THIS QUESTION BECAUSE THE DEMON OF A DRUG ADDICTION
CAN ONLY BE CAST OUT BY USING GOD'S WORDS WHILE HE IS
IN THE ADDICTION.*

SATAN'S TRIANGLE

UNDERSTAND YOU! FOR THIS DEMON IS A CLEVER DEVIL, AND HE'S THE OPPOSITE OF YOU. THAT'S WHY HE MAKES A FOOL OUT YOU EVERYTIME YOU USE DRUGS. HE HAS YOU HALF-CRAZY, SCARED, AND OUT OF YOUR MIND. HE HAS YOU FIGHTING WIFE, CHILDREN, FAMILY, AND FRIENDS. YET, IN HIS DEPARTURE, HE'LL LEAVE YOU BROKE, SCARED, OR IN BONDAGE. WOE! OF COURSE, BY YOU BEING THE ONE IN JAIL YOU WILL THINK IT IS YOU, BUT ALL THE TIME IT IS YOUR ADDICTION, WHICH IS THE DEVIL. THEREFORE, IT TAKES GOD TO DELIVER YOU FROM THE DEMON OF THIS ADDICTION, FOR YOU CAN'T FIGHT SATAN'S EVIL TRIANGLE IN THIS THREE DIMENSIONAL THING. THUS, THE DEVIL, DRUGS, AND HIS DEMONS. FOR WE ALL HAVE OUR OWN DEMONS, BUT IN YOUR ADDICTION YOU HAVE MANY. WOE!

CALL THE LORD

UNDERSTAND YOU! IN ORDER TO CAST THE DEMON OUT OF A DRUG ADDICTION, RIGHT AFTER YOU FEEL THE AFFECT OF THE DRUGS, IMMEDIATELY, CALL ON THE LORD TO DELIVER YOU! THIS UNIMAGINABLE, UNDESCRIBABLE, AND UNBELIEVABLE DEVILISH, GOOD FEELING IS THE DEMON OF A DRUG ADDICTION. (your high) YOU CAN'T FIGHT THIS ORGASMIC FEELING BECAUSE THE DEMON OF THIS ADDICTION WILL BE IN YOU. YET, WHEN YOU CALL ON THE LORD, GOD'S WORDS BREAK THE YOKE OF THESE DEVILS WHILE THEY ARE STILL WITHIN THE SPIRITUAL WORLD OF YOUR SUBCONSCIOUS MIND. THIS IS A WELL KEPT SECRET, BUT NOW IT IS ONLY KNOWN BY YOU. THOSE WHO CALLED ON THE LORD DELIVERED THEMSELVES FROM THEIR ADDICTIONS WHILE THEY WERE HIGH. YET, TO THIS DAY, THEY STILL DO NOT KNOW HOW THEY WERE DELIVERED. OF COURSE, THEY DO KNOW THAT IT WAS NOBODY BUT GOD THAT DELIVERED THEM. THUS, NOW YOU KNOW AND YOU MUST UNDERSTAND THIS MYSTERY. FOR YOU WILL BE OVERWHELMED BY THESE

DEVILISH, GOOD FEELINGS; THESE DEMONS WILL HAVE YOU WANTING MORE DRUGS, AND MORE DRUGS, AND MORE DRUGS UNTIL THE DEVIL DECEIVES YOU UNTO DEATH. ARE YOU LISTENING TO YOU?

HIGH OVER, DEMON GONE

THEN UNDERSTAND YOU! WHEN YOUR HIGH IS OVER, THE DEMON WILL LEAVE THE ADDICTION, AND YOU CAN NOT CAST THE DEMON OUT OF A DRUG ADDICTION ONCE THE DEMON HAS LEFT. YOU CAN NOT CAST THE DEMON OUT OF A DRUG ADDICTION ONCE YOUR HIGH IS OVER AND YOU CAN NOT CAST THE DEMON OUT OF A DRUG ADDICTION WHEN YOU ARE BACK TO YOUR NORMAL SELF (conscious). THE DEMON LEFT THE ADDICTION THE MOMENT THE HIGH LEFT THE ADDICTION AND WHATEVER YOU DO AFTER THE DEMON LEAVES THE ADDICTION WILL DO YOU NO GOOD. WHAT GOOD WILL IT DO YOU THEN TO CALL ON THE LORD WHEN THE HIGH IS OVER AND THE DEMON IS GONE? FOR YOU'RE FIENDING, BUT ARE YOU HIGH? IF SO, THE DEMON IS STILL WITHIN THE ADDICTION, BUT SINCE YOU ARE NOT HIGH, HE IS GONE! DO YOU UNDERSTAND? YOUR HIGH IS THE DEMON OF THIS ADDICTION AND HE CAN ONLY BE CAST OUT WHILE HE IS IN THE ADDICTION. WHEN YOU ARE NOT HIGH, THERE IS NO DEMON TO BE CAST OUT OF THE ADDICTION. YOU ARE YOU! DO YOU NOT UNDERSTAND THIS DARK SAYING?

UNDERSTAND YOU BEFORE THIS DEMON GETS AWAY. HE IS TRICKY IN THIS ADDICTION AND THAT IS WHY YOU CAN ONLY CAST HIM OUT WHILE HE'S IN THE ADDICTION (high). YET, YOU ARE NOT HIGH ON DRUGS ARE YOU? NOPE! ARE YOU IN THE SPIRITUAL WORLD OF YOUR SUBCONSCIOUS MIND? NOPE! YOU ARE BACK INTO YOUR CONSCIOUS STATE OF MIND. YES! WHERE IS THE DEMON TO BE CAST OUT? THE DEMON IS YOUR ADDICTION ONLY WHEN YOU ARE HIGH, BUT YOU ARE NOT HIGH. DO YOU NOW SEE THIS DEVIL? THE DEMON LEAVES THE

ADDICTION WHEN THE HIGH LEAVES THE ADDICTION AND WHEN YOU ARE NOT USING DRUGS HE IS GONE. DO YOU SEE THE LIGHT?

SHED LIGHT ON DEMON

LET US SHED MORE LIGHT ON THIS DEVIL BECAUSE THE DEMON OF A DRUG ADDICTION WILL ONLY COME WHEN YOU ARE USING DRUGS AND NOT WHEN YOU ARE SOBER! YOU ARE NOT ADDICTED TO A DRUG UNTIL YOU USE THE DRUG. THEN, AND ONLY THEN, ARE YOU ADDICTED TO THAT DRUG AT THAT PARTICULAR TIME AND ONLY DURING THAT PARTICULAR HIGH OF THE MOMENT. FOR YOU HAVE ALLOWED YOURSELF TO USE THE DRUGS AND THE DEMON OF THAT ADDICTION WILL ONLY COME WHEN YOU ARE IN THE SPIRITUAL WORLD OF YOUR SUBCONSCIOUS MIND WHERE THE DEVIL AWAITS YOU. WOE! YET, YOU ARE NOT HIGH, ARE YOU? NO! AFRAID? YES! BUT HIGH? NOT WHEN YOU'RE SOBER.

WHEN DEMONS LEAVE ADDICTIONS

UNDERSTAND YOU! WHEN THE DEMON LEAVES THE ADDICTION, GOING TO REHAB WILL DO YOU NO GOOD. WHAT DEMON DID YOU TAKE TO REHAB WITH YOU OTHER THAN YOU? THE DEMONIC SPIRIT WILL BE WAITING IN THE ADDICTION WHEN YOU RETURN FROM REHAB. YOU ARE THE ONE WHO WENT TO REHAB, NOT THE DEMON! THE DEMON IS IN THE ADDICTION, NOT YOU! THEREFORE, GOING TO REHAB WILL KEEP THE DEMON OUT OF THE ADDICTION BECAUSE THERE IS NO ADDICTION IN REHAB. YOU ARE NOT USING DRUGS; YOU ARE IN A SECURE PLACE AND YOU HAVE NOT GOTTEN HIGH. THE DEMON IS NOT IN REHAB WITH YOU UNLESS YOU ARE IN REHAB USING DRUGS. UNDERSTAND YOU! THIS DEMON'S JOB IS TO KEEP YOU ADDICTED UNTIL THE DAY YOU DIE. WHEREFORE, HIS ADDICTION IS YOUR USAGE AND YOUR USAGE IS HIS ADDICTION. HE CAN'T LIVE WITHOUT YOU USING DRUGS AND SATAN HAS GIVEN HIM THE POWER OF HELL TO KEEP YOU ADDICTED.

DEMON LIFE IN ADDICTION

THE LIFE OF A DRUG-ADDICTED DEMON IS IN ADDICTION. YET, YOU ARE NOT FIGHTING AN ADDICTION BECAUSE YOU ARE NOT ADDICTED! YOU ARE FIGHTING THE DEMON WITHIN THIS ADDICTION AND YOU WILL STILL USE DRUGS WHEN YOU GET OUT OF REHAB BECAUSE THE DEMON WILL STILL BE WITHIN THE ADDICTION. DO YOU NOT UNDERSTAND? YOU HAVE NOT DELIVERED YOURSELF BY CALLING ON THE LORD WHILE THE DEMON WAS YET WITHIN THE ADDICTION. THUS, YOU JUST GOT HIGH, FREAKY, AND ENJOYED THE DRUGS. BUT YOU HAVE TO USE THE SCRIPTURE ON THESE DEVILS IN ORDER FOR GOD TO CAST THEM OUT OF DRUGS. THAT IS HOW YOU STOP USING DRUGS BY ALLOWING GOD TO CAST THE DEMON OUT THE HIGH OF THIS ADDICTION WHILE YOU ARE USING DRUGS. GOD'S WORDS TRAP THE DEMON WITHIN THIS ADDICTION BECAUSE WHEN YOU USE DRUGS YOU ARE NOT YOU, YOU ARE IN THE SPIRITUAL WORLD OF YOUR SUBCONSCIOUS MIND. WHILE YOU ARE HIGH, GOD'S WORD IS THE LAST THING THESE DEVILS WILL EVER EXPECT COMING FROM YOU. YET, GOD SAID, "FOR MY PEOPLE PERISH FROM LACK OF KNOWLEDGE" (Hosea 4: 6).

GOOD YOU WENT TO REHAB

YOU JUST TOOK A BREAK FROM YOUR DAILY USAGE BY GOING TO REHAB (safe heaven) AND IT WAS A GOOD THING THAT YOU WENT. PERHAPS, HAD YOU NOT WENT AT THE TIME YOU WENT, YOU WOULD HAVE BEEN DEAD. GOD MOVES IN MYSTERIOUS WAYS AND HIS WAY IS NOT YOUR WAY. HIS THOUGHTS ARE NOT YOUR THOUGHTS, AND HIS WORDS ARE NOT YOUR WORDS (Isaiah 55: 8-9). GOD DELIVERED YOU THEN BECAUSE THE DEVIL WAS ABOUT TO LOCK YOU INTO YOUR SUBCONSCIOUS MIND AND THAT IS WHY YOU WENT TO REHAB. GOD MADE IT POSSIBLE FOR YOU TO ESCAPE DEATH BY GOING TO REHAB IN ORDER TO BREAK THE CYCLE OF THAT DEADLY ADDICTION. AN ADDICTION IS AN ADDICTION EVERY TIME YOU USE DRUGS, BUT NEVER IS AN ADDICTION THE SAME

ADDICTION. EVEN THOUGH YOU ARE USING THE SAME DRUGS, IT IS A DIFFERENT ADDICTION. THE DEVIL IN HIS DECEPTION KEEPS YOU ADDICTED TO DRUGS BECAUSE A DRUG ADDICTION IS DIABOLICAL. DIFFERENT DEMONS COME AND GO. THE SAME AS THE 999 CHANGES OF AN ADDICTION YOU WILL GO THROUGH TURNED UP-SIDE DOWN. WHICH EVER WAY YOU LOOK AT IT, IT WILL STILL COME TO 666. THE DEVIL! FOR AN ADDICTION IS AN ADDICTION AS LONG AS THERE IS A DEMON WITHIN THE ADDICTION.

POLICE THE DEMON

THERE WAS A CERTAIN MAN WHO GOT HIGH AND CALLED THE POLICE ON HIMSELF. THE DEMON WITHIN THE ADDICTION SCARED THE MAN. YET, WHEN THE OFFICERS ARRIVED, THE MAN WAS BACK TO HIS NORMAL SELF. THE DEMONIC SPIRIT HAD LEFT THE MAN, BUT THE OFFICERS KNEW HE WAS HIGH ON DRUGS WHEN HE CALLED THE POLICE. THUS, UNDERSTAND YOU! ONCE THE DEMON LEAVES THE ADDICTION, CALLING ON GOD AFTERWARDS WILL DO YOU NO GOOD. THE SAME AS IT WAS WITH THE MAN WHO CALLED THE POLICE ON HIMSELF. WHAT GOOD WILL IT DO YOU THEN TO CALL GOD WHEN THE WICKED SPIRIT IS NO LONGER WITHIN THE ADDICTION? ONCE THE DEMONIC SPIRIT LEAVES THE ADDICTION, YOU CAN POUT AND STAY ON YOUR PITY POT AS LONG AS YOU LIKE, BUT IT WILL DO YOU NO GOOD. THE DAMAGE BY THE DEMON WAS BEING DONE WHILE YOU WERE USING DRUGS AND THAT IS THE TIME YOU SHOULD HAVE CALLED GOD, WHEN THE DEMON WAS YET WITHIN THE ADDICTION (high). YOUR DELIVERANCE OF AN ADDICTION WOULD COME FROM GOD WHILE THE WICKED SPIRIT IS STILL WITHIN YOU.

THE MIND'S EYE

UNDERSTAND YOU BEFORE YOU CLOSE THE MIND'S EYE AND NOT SEE WHAT THE SPIRIT IS TRYING TO CONVEY TO YOU.

WHEN THE DEMON LEAVES THE ADDICTION, CALLING ON GOD AFTER THE DEMONIC SPIRIT HAS LEFT WOULD BE TO MINISTER TO THE DAMAGE DONE BY THE DEMON WHILE HE WAS YET IN YOU, BUT NOT NECESSARILY TOWARDS YOUR DELIVERANCE. RIGHT NOW, STOP AND WALK OUT THE FRONT DOOR OF YOUR HOUSE. YOU ARE ON THE OUTSIDE LOOKING IN. WHAT CAN YOU DO ABOUT THE DEMON INSIDE THE HOUSE? NOTHING! EXACTLY, NOW GO BACK INTO YOUR HOME. WHAT CAN YOU DO ABOUT THE DEMON WITHOUT? NOTHING! EXACTLY. THE DEMONIC SPIRIT OF AN ADDICTION WILL ONLY APPEAR WHEN YOU ARE IN THE SPIRITUAL WORLD OF YOUR SUBCONSCIOUS MIND AND THAT'S WHEN THE WICKED SPIRIT IS WITHIN THE HOUSE. YOU MUST CALL ON THE LORD RIGHT THEN WHILE THE WICKED SPIRIT IS STILL WITHIN THE ADDICTION. THE LORD WILL CAST THAT DEMONIC SPIRIT OUT OF THAT ADDICTION WHILE HE'S YET IN THE ADDICTION (you). DO YOU UNDERSTAND THIS SIMPLE PROCESS OR DOES SATAN HAVE TO SCARE THE HELL OUT OF YOU TO CALL ON THE LORD? GOOD GOD ALMIGHTY! WHEN YOU CALL ON THE LORD, THE DEMONIC SPIRIT WITHIN THAT ADDICTION WILL DISAPPEAR, BUT THEY ARE A LEGION. (Mark 5: 9- 10)

SATAN SENDS ANOTHER DEMON

THEREFORE, EVERY TIME YOUR DEMONIC CRAVINGS DECEIVE YOU INTO GETTING HIGH, SATAN WILL SEND ANOTHER DEMON. YOU MUST USE GOD'S WORDS TO FIGHT THE DEMONIC SPIRITS OF THAT ADDICTION. YOU DON'T KNOW THIS, BUT THE DEVIL KNOWS ONCE YOU'RE HIGH, YOU WILL ENJOY THE DRUGS AND FORGET ABOUT THE WORD OF GOD. THUS FAR, HE'S BEEN RIGHT ABOUT YOU. YET, HE'S A LIE, AND THE FATHER OF A LIE (John 8:44). GOD'S WORDS ARE STRONGER THAN DRUGS AND EVERY DEVIL IN HELL BOWS DOWN TO THE WORD OF GOD (James 2:19). SO SHOULD YOU. THE WORD OF GOD HELPS YOU WITHSTAND THE WILES AND WOES OF THE DEVIL WHILE YOU'RE IN THE SPIRITUAL WORLD OF YOUR SUBCONSCIOUS MIND (Ephesians 6:11). BLACK SHEEP, BY THE

SELF RIGHTEOUSNESS OF YOU AND YOUR TRYING EFFORTS TO STOP USING DRUGS, GOD WILL DELIVER YOU FROM THE DEMON OF A DRUG ADDICTION WHEN YOU CALL ON THE LORD.

ARMOR OF GOD

NOW, UNDERSTAND YOU! BY KNOWING HOW AND WHEN TO CAST THE DEMON OUT OF A DRUG ADDICTION, THE DEMON IS AFRAID OF YOU AND IN YOUR ADDICTION HE KNOWS YOU WLL CALL ON THE LORD. THE DEMON KNOWS YOU HAVE PUT ON THE FULL ARMOR OF GOD AND THE WORD OF GOD PROTECTS YOU (Ephesians 6:10-18). GOD KNOWS YOU WANT TO STOP USING DRUGS, BUT THESE DEMONS IN THE ADDICTION KEEP YOU ADDICTED TO DRUGS. GOD KNOWS THAT YOU HATE DRUGS, BUT THESE DEMONS IN THE ADDICTION LOVE DRUGS. GOD KNOWS THAT YOU ARE TIRED OF USING DRUGS, BUT THE DEMON IN THE ADDICTION WILL KEEP YOU SAD IF HE DOES NOT GET HIS DRUGS. THEREFORE, BY YOU KNOWING WHEN TO CAST THE DEMONIC SPIRITS OUT OF THE ADDICTION THIS IS "HOW YOU STOP USING DRUGS." WHEN? EVERY TIME ONE OF THESE SAD DEMONS DECEIVES YOU INTO USING DRUGS,CALL ON THE LORD AND GOD'S WORDS WILL BREAK THE YOKE OF THEIR DEMONIC ADDICTION. "FOR THE WORD OF GOD IS QUICK AND POWERFUL, AND SHARPER THAN ANY TWO-EDGED SWORD, PIERCING EVEN TO THE DIVIDING ASUNDER OF SOUL AND SPIRIT, AND OF THE JOINTS AND MARROW, AND IS A DISCERNER OF THE THOUGHTS AND INTENTS OF THE HEART" (Hebrews 4:12).

RELAPSE PART OF RECOVERY

GOD'S WORD IS POWER, YET RELAPSE IS A PART OF YOUR RECOVERY. THAT IS BECAUSE EVERY TIME GOD CASTS OUT A DEMON, SATAN WILL SEND ANOTHER DEMON. NOT BECAUSE HE GIVES A DAMN, BUT BECAUSE HE'S THE DEVIL. SATAN DOES NOT WANT TO LOSE THIS SUBLIMINAL WAR WITH GOD OVER

YOUR SOUL IN THE SPIRITUAL WORLD OF YOUR SUBCONSCIOUS MIND. THEREFORE, EVERY TIME YOU RELAPSE, YOU ARE A DOOR AWAY FROM DEATH. WOE! THE DEAD ARE CALLING YOU AND IT IS TIME TO PAY THE PIPER. SATAN WANTS YOUR SOUL, BUT GOD SAYS HE CAN NOT HAVE IT. NOT SO! THEREFFORE, WHEN YOU RELAPSE YOU CAN NOT SEE YOUR FACE THE MORNING AFTER AND YOU HATE THE THINGS YOU'VE DONE THE NIGHT BEFORE. WOE! THEN, YOU WILL CALL ON THE LORD TO DELIVER YOU FROM DRUGS AFTER YOU HAVE ENJOYED USING DRUGS. THEN YOU WILL CALL ON THE LORD TO DELIVER YOU FROM DRUGS, EVEN THOUGH YOU ARE NOT TRYING TO STOP USING DRUGS. AND THEN YOU WILL CALL ON THE LORD TO DELIVER YOU FROM DRUGS, BUT NOT FROM YOUR UNGODLY WAYS. HE IS NOT A GOD THAT ENTERTAINS DEVILS. HE IS A GOD THAT CASTS OUT DEVILS AND IF YOU PRAY HARD ENOUGH HE'LL KEEP YOU FROM BECOMING ONE. WOE!

HATING RELAPSE

HOWEVER, BY YOU HATING YOURSELF EVERY TIME YOU RELAPSE, YOU SHOULD BE AWARE THAT YOU ARE ON THE THRESHOLD OF YOUR RECOVERY. WHEN YOU CHANGE THE METHOD OF HOW YOU USE DRUGS, ALL OF A SUDDEN, A CHANGE WILL COME OVER YOU. UNBEKNOWNST TO YOU, GOD WILL DELIVER YOU THROUGH YOUR CONSTANT PRAYERS WHILE DRUGS ARE STILL IN YOUR MOUTH AND THE DEVIL'S LIES ARE RUNNING THROUGH YOUR VEINS, NOT EVEN YOU WILL KNOW WHY YOU DON'T WANT ANY MORE DRUGS. FOR YOU WILL UNDERSTAND WHEN YOU HAVE CHANGED YOUR WICKED WAYS AND STARTED USING GOD'S WORDS. GOD DELIVERED YOU FROM THE DEMON OF A DRUG ADDICTION. GOOD GOD ALMIGHTY! THE TASTE FOR DRUGS ARE NO LONGER ON THE TIP OF YOUR TONGUE AND YOUR CRAVINGS FOR DRUGS ARE NO LONGER IN THE MIND. YOU DON'T KNOW IT, BUT YOU WERE BEING DELIVERED BY GOD FROM THE DEMON OF THIS ADDICTION WHILE YOU WERE HIGH, SCARED, AND USING DRUGS. GOOD GOD ALMIGHTY!

USING DRUGS TO BE DELIVERED

IRONICALLY, THE MYSTERY OF A DRUG ADDICTION IS THAT YOU HAVE TO USE DRUGS TO BE DELIVERED FROM DRUGS. HOW CAN YOU BE ADDICTED TO A DRUG YOU'VE NEVER USED? A DRUG YOU HAVE NEVER TASTED? A DRUG YOU'VE NEVER TAKEN? YOU WILL NOT KNOW IT, BUT GOD WAS CASTING DEMONS OUT OF YOUR ADDICTION EVERYTIME YOU USED DRUGS. YOU WILL NOT EVEN KNOW WHEN, WHERE, WHY, OR HOW YOU WERE BEING DELIVERED, BUT NOW YOU KNOW. GOD WAS DELIVERING YOU IN YOUR DRUGGAFIED STATE WHILE YOU WERE IN THE SPIRITUAL WORLD OF YOUR SUBCONSCIOUS MIND. YOU UNCONSCIOUSLY WERE CASTING OUT DEMONS BY USING GOD'S WORDS EVERY TIME YOU GOT HIGH, BUT YOUR ADDICTION WAS BEYOND YOUR UNDERSTANDING. YET, YOU DELIVERED YOURSELF EVERY TIME YOU CALLED ON THE LORD FOR YOUR DELIVERANCE. THUS, BY THE WORD OF GOD THAT BE IN YOU, THE WORDS OF GOD DELIVERED YOU. HALLELUJAH! FOR HE'S A GOOD GOD! HE MADE THE MOUTH NOT WANT TO TASTE ANY MORE DRUGS,AND SINCE THE DEMONS ARE NO LONGER IN THE ADDICTION, THE MIND WILL NEVER MISS IT. WHAT A GOD! THANK YOU JESUS OF NAZARETH! FOR THY SAVING GRACE FROM THE DEMONS OF A DRUG ADDICTION! THE DEMON WITHIN A DRUG ADDICTION WAS BEING CAST OUT BY THE WORD OF GOD WHILE YOU WERE GETTING HIGH AND USING DRUGS. THUS, BY YOU USING GOD'S WORDS AS YOU USED DRUGS EVERY TIME YOU GOT HIGH, GOD DESTROYED THOSE DEVILS AND THEIR DEMONIC ADDICTIONS ARE NO MORE. YOU HAVE BEEN DELIVERED. HALLELUJAH!

DELIVERANCE COME FROM UNDERSTANDING

YOU UNDERSTAND THE MYSTERY OF A DRUG ADDICTION. THEN UNDERSTAND YOU! YOU PERSONALLY, WERE BEING DELIVERED BY GOD FROM THE DEMONS WITHIN YOUR ADDICTION. WHATSOEVER BE YOUR ADDICTION AS AN ADDICTION, GOD HAS GAUGED THAT ADDICTION TO THE

*HEART OF THIS MATTER. THUS, YOUR PRAYERS ARE ANSWERED
AND YOUR HEART'S CONFESSION GOD HAS HEARD. GOD KNOWS
EVERYTHING ABOUT YOU AND THERE IS NOTHING ABOUT YOU
THAT WAS NOT ALREADY KNOWN BY THE CREATOR OF YOU, FOR
GOD KNOWS EXACTLY WHAT HE MADE WHEN HE CREATED YOU!
CAN THE CREATION SAY TO THE CREATOR, "WHAT MAKETH
THOU YOU?" (Isaiah 45:18) YOU ARE WHICH EVER YOU ARE AND
GOD SAYS COME AS YOU ARE. ARE YOU NOT YOU? YOU ARE
NOTHING LESS THAN GOD'S CREATION AND WITH 90 DEGREE
KNOWLEDGE OF A DIVINE INTERVENTION, YOU SHOULD HAVE
FELT YOUR DELIVERANCE. HALLELUJAH!*

SATAN YOKE BROKEN

*THE DEVIL CAN NOT DECEIVE YOU ANYMORE WITH HIS
DEMONIC ADDICTION. THE WORDS OF GOD SPOKEN IN DUE
SEASON BREAKS THE YOKE OF THE DEVIL IN ALL ADDICTIONS.
THE DEMON ASSIGNED TO THIS ADDICTION WAS CAST OUT IN
THE NAME OF THE LORD WHILE YOU WERE USING DRUGS.
THEY ARE NO MORE IN THE ADDICTION BECAUSE GOD HAS
DELIVERED YOU FROM DRUGS. SATAN IS A LIE AND THE
FATHER OF A LIE, BUT NOW YOU KNOW THE TRUTH. THUS,
ONLY GOD CAN DELIVER YOU FROM THE EVIL OF HIS OWN
CREATION AND FROM SUCH AN EVIL HAS GOD DELIVERED YOU
FROM THE DEMON OF A DRUGS ADDICTION. HALLELUJAH!*

POWER OF SALVATION

*FOR THEY ARE NO MORE SAITH THE LORD AND THANK YOU
LORD, HALLELUJAH! PRAISE THE LORD FOR THY DELIVERANCE.
GO THY WAY IN PEACE THY BELOVED BROTHERS AND SISTERS
IN CHRIST AND UNDERSTAND YOU! THE LORD HAS SPOKEN ON
ADDICTION AS DEMONIC! YOU ALONE CAN NOT DELIVER
YOUSELF FROM THE DEMON OF A DRUG ADDICTION. ONLY
GOD'S WORD CAN DELIVER YOU FROM THE DEMON OF AN
ADDICTION! THEREFORE, BE NOT ASHAMED BY THE GOSPEL*

OF JESUS CHRIST, FOR IT IS THE POWER OF GOD UNTO SALVATION TO EVERY ONE THAT BELIEVETH; TO THE JEW FIRST, AND ALSO TO THE GREEK (Romans 1:16).

DELIVERANCE FROM ADDICTION

FOR YOU SHOULD BE REJOICING BECAUSE THE DEMONS ARE RELUCTANT TO ENTER INTO THE SPIRITUAL WARFARE OF THEIR ADDICTIONS WHENEVER YOU USE DRUGS. YET, THEY HAVE NO OTHER CHOICE, BUT TO GO INTO YOUR SUBCONSCIOUS MIND WHENEVER YOU GET HIGH, FOR THEY KNOW YOU HAVE BECOME WISE IN YOUR ADDICTION AND THE WORD OF GOD SUSTAINS YOU. YOU HAVE ARMED YOUSELF WITH GOD'S WORDS AND THE DRUGS ARE NO LONGER ON TOP OF YOU. IN OTHER WORDS, YOU ARE NOT AS DUMB, NAIVE, AND GULLIBLE AS YOU ONCE WERE BEFORE YOU STARTED USING GOD'S WORDS. THE DEMONS TRIED LIKE HELL TO KILL YOU AND THEY WANTED TO SCARE YOUR FRIGHTENED LITTLE SOUL TO DEATH, BUT THROUGH IT ALL, GOD HAS ALWAYS BEEN THERE TO PROTECT YOU. THEY KNOW THIS, BUT NOW WHEN YOU USE DRUGS, THESE DEMONS FLEE FROM YOUR ADDICTION AS THEY FLEE FOR THEIR LIFE. FOR YOUR TEMPLE (body) BECAME A HOLY SANCTUARY UNTO THEM (1Corinthians 3: 16). THUS, UNINHABITABLE FOR DEMONIC HABITATIONS. THE DEMONS WERE TRAPPED WITHIN THE SPIRITUAL WORLD OF YOUR SUBCONSCIOUS MIND BY THE WORD OF GOD WHEN YOU WERE IN YOUR DRUGGAFIED STATE AND THEY CAN NOT SURVIVE NOR ESCAPE THEIR FATE (Hebrews 2:14-15)!

WHAT THE DEMONS THOUGHT

THE DEMONS THOUGHT WHEN YOU HIT THE PIPE, SATAN WAS GOING TO LOCK YOU INTO YOUR SUBCONSCIOUS MIND. THEY THOUGHT WHEN YOU USED THE DRUGS, THEIR DADDY WAS GOING TO SCARE YOU TO DEATH. AND THEY KNEW AFTER THAT

BIG HIT, YOU SHALL SURELY DIE. BUT AS SOON AS YOU FELT THE AFFECT OF THE DRUGS. YOU FOOLED THESE DEVILS! YOU STARTED REBUKING THEM IN CHRIST'S NAME, QUOTING SCRIPTURES AND CALLING ON THE LORD (Matthew 16:23)(Matthew 4:10)(Luke 4:1-13)! THESE DEVILS WERE SURPRISED AT YOU, BUT FOR THEM IT WAS TOO LATE! GOD'S WORDS DELIVERED YOU AS IT DESTROYED THEIR DEMONIC YOKE AND FREED YOU FROM THE DEMONS OF THAT ADDICTION. THEIR ADDICTION WAS CAST OUT BY THE BIBILICAL KNOWLEDGE OF THE GOD IN YOU. USING GOD'S WORDS TO FIGHT THESE DEMONS, YOU OVER CAME THAT DEMONIC ADDICTION AND NOW THESE DEMONS ARE AFRAID OF YOU. THEY KNOW YOU KNOW WHAT TO DO. THEY KNOW ONCE YOU GET HIGH, YOU WILL GET SCARED AND THEN CALL ON THE LORD AND GOD'S WORDS WILL DESTROY THEM AS IT DELIVERS YOU.

YOU GETTING HIGH BY YOURSELF

MY LORD! THANKS BE TO GOD THAT DRUGS NO LONGER TASTE THE SAME IN YOUR MOUTH BECAUSE WHENEVER YOU GET HIGH, YOU ARE GETTING HIGH BY YOURSELF. GOD IS WATCHING OVER YOU AND HE'S ALLOWING YOU TO GO BACK TO THE DAYS BEFORE YOUR ADDICTION TO SEE IF YOU REALLY WANT DRUGS. GOD KNOWS, BUT YOU DO NOT KNOW YOU STOPPED USING DRUGS WITHOUT DEMONIC INTERFERENCE. SATAN KNOWS YOU HAVE BECOME WISE IN THE ADDICTION AND HIS DEMONS KNOW YOU ARE BEING PROTECTED BY GOD. YOU HAVE STARTED LOOKING BETTER, DRESSING BETTER, AND DOING WELL. SATAN KNOWS AT ONE TIME IN YOUR ADDICTION, YOU WERE AFRAID OF THESE DEVILS. THEY HAD YOU RUNNING DOWN THE STREETS HALF-NAKED, HIDING UNDER BEDS, IN CLOSETS, BATHROOMS, AND TOO AFRAID TO LEAVE YOUR OWN HOUSE. WOE! BUT NOW, HIS DEMONS ARE AFRAID OF YOUR ADDICTION SINCE YOU HAVE INCLUDED GOD IN YOUR HIGH. THEIR HIGH! THUS, THE DEVIL'S DEMON WAS ASSIGNED TO THIS "HIGH" UNTIL GOD SHOWED UP AND NOW THEY ARE BEING DESTROYED BY THE WORD OF GOD EVERY

TIME YOU USED DRUGS. GOD WILL NOT ALLOW ANY OF THESE LITTLE DEVILS TO ESCAPE THEIR FATE. WHENEVER THEY COME INTO THE SPIRITUAL WORLD OF YOUR SUBCONSCIOUS MIND, EVERY TIME YOU CALLED ON THE LORD, YOU DESTROYED THEIR ADDICTIONS. THIS IS A MYSTERY AND THE DEVIL KEPT SECRET. THEY HAVE KEPT THIS SECRET AND YOU ADDICTED LONG ENOUGH BEFORE YOU LEARNED TO USE GOD'S WORDS ON THESE DEVILS. THEIR ADDICTION WAS FOR YOUR SOUL. YET, YOU THOUGHT IT WAS FOR YOUR HIGH AND THAT IS WHY SATAN GAVE YOU MORE DRUGS AND MORE DRUGS AND MORE DRUGS. HE GAVE YOU DRUGS FOR YOUR SOUL AND EVERY TIME YOU THOUGHT YOU GOT HIGH, YOU WERE LIKE A FROG EATING HOT COALS (Revelation 16: 13). MY GOD!

GOD'S ANGELS FIGHTING SATAN FOR YOUR SOUL

GOD ANGELS ARE FIGHTING SATAN AND HIS ARMY OF DEMONS IN THE SPIRITUAL WORLD OF YOUR SUBCONSCIOUS MIND AND YOU DO NOT EVEN HAVE A CLUE THAT SUCH A WAR IS TAKING PLACE WITHIN YOU. HOWEVER, WHEN YOU STOP USING DRUGS FOR A SHORT WHILE, AND WITHOUT GOD'S DELIVERANCE YOU WILL BRING BACK INTO THE ADDICTION SEVEN MORE WICKED SPIRITS FAR WORSE THAN THE FIRST (Matthew 12:45). WOE! A DRUG ADDICTION CAN HAVE A THOUSAND DEMONS IN IT DEPENDING ON HOW MANY TIMES YOU HAVE STOPPED AND STARTED BACK USING DRUGS. YOU HAVE GOD PROTECTING YOU, BUT BECAUSE HE'S THE DEVIL AND MAKES DEMONS EVERY DAY, SATAN CARES NO MORE FOR THESE DEMONS THAT GOD'S DESTROYING THAN HE DOES FOR YOU. SATAN WANTS YOUR SOUL AND HE WILL TRY EVERY TRICK IN HELL TO GET IT.

SATAN'S DEMONS MUST FIGHT

THEREFORE, HIS DEMONS HAVE NO OTHER CHOICE, BUT TO GO TO BATTLE WITH THE SPIRIT OF GOD IN YOUR SUBCONSCIOUS MIND EVERY TIME YOU USE DRUGS. BELEIVE IT OR NOT, THESE

DEVILS HOPE YOU MESS UP AND STOP USING DRUGS. GOD IS DESTROYING THEIR ADDICTION EVERY TIME YOU GET HIGH. BECAUSE THE DEMONS ARE ASSIGNED TO THIS ADDICTION, THEY MUST DO AS THEIR MASTER SAYS. THEY HAVE TO GO INTO WAR AGAINST GOD WITHIN THE SPIRITUAL WORLD OF YOUR SUBCONSCIOUS MIND WHENEVER YOU GET HIGH. THE SAME WAY SATAN MAKES YOU THINK YOU HAVE NO OTHER CHOICE IN THEIR ADDICTION, BUT TO USE DRUGS. SO YOU DO! MY GOD, WHAT AN ADDICTION! THE DEMON AND YOU HAVE SOMETHING IN COMMON. YOU USE DRUGS TO GET HIGH AND THE DEMON KEEPS YOU ADDICTED IN ORDER TO LIVE. THE REASON THE LITTLE IMPS ARE RELUCTANT TO ENTER YOUR HIGH IS BECAUSE THEY SAY NOW YOU CALL ON THE LORD TOO MUCH. MY GOD! THEY SAY YOU ALWAYS TALK ABOUT GOD AS SOON AS YOU GET HIGH. GOOD! THEY SAY NO ONE CAN STAND TO BE AROUND YOU WHEN YOU USE DRUGS. GREAT! FOR THESE LITTLE IMPS HAVE STIGMATIZED YOU AND YOU HAVE BEEN OSTRACIZED BY OTHER ADDICTS CONTROLLED BY SATAN (friends). YET, IT SHOULD MAKE YOU HAPPY KNOWING YOU ARE THE ANOINTED ONE OF GOD. YOU SHOULD BE HAPPY YOU HAVE FOUND THE GOD IN YOU! SATAN IN THIS WAR WITH GOD OVER YOUR SOUL WILL WITHDRAW HIS FEW DEMONS THAT ARE LEFT BEFORE GOD DESTROYS THEM ALL. OUR GOD IS ALMIGHTY! SATAN ALONE WITH HIS DEMONS WILL ACCEPT DEFEAT THE SAME AS HE DID WITH CHRIST ON CALVARY (1 Corinthians 15:57) AND YOUR DEMONIC ADDICTION WILL BE NO MORE. THUS, SAITH THE LORD (Isaiah 44:6). HALLELUJAH!

SATAN ACCEPT DEFEAT

IN KNOWING THAT HE HAS LOST THE WAR ON DRUGS IN THE SPIRITUAL WORLD OF YOUR SUBCONSCIOUS MIND, SATAN WILL TAKE HIS DEMONS BEFORE GOD DESTROYS HIM ALONG WITH THESE DEVILS AND LOOK FOR ANOTHER YOU. PERHAPS, ONE OF YOUR TURN-OUTS BECAUSE SATAN KNOWS YOU HAVE USED DRUGS PER SE AND THE DEMONS OF YOUR ADDICTION HAVE KEPT YOU ADDICTED UNTIL YOU FOUND THE LORD.

SATAN ISN'T JUST ANY FOOL. HE'S THE KING OF FOOLS AND THE FATHER OF A LIE. HE KNOWS YOU HAVE FOUND THE LORD AND HE'S NOT FOOLISH ENOUGH TO LOSE HIS ARMY IN A WAR WITH GOD OVER A LOST SOUL. YOU WERE A LOST SOUL, BUT NOW YOU ARE FOUNDED BY THE GOSPEL OF JESUS CHRIST THAT BE IN YOU (Luke 15: 1-32). SATAN KNOWS THERE IS NO OTHER WAY IN HELL YOU CAN ESCAPE FROM THE DEMONS OF A DRUG ADDICTION WITHOUT GOD. HE KNOWS YOUR DELIVERANCE FROM A DRUG-USING DEMON CAN ONLY COME FROM GOD. YOU HAVE BECOME HOLY AND HE KNOWS IT. BECAUSE IT IS IMPOSSIBLE FOR YOU TO STOP USING DRUGS ON YOUR OWN AND WITHOUT GOD. SATAN KNEW THE MINUTE YOU WERE PIPE-BITTEN AND THE VERY HOUR YOU WEANED YOURSELF OFF THE DEVIL'S HORN. HE KNEW THE DAY OF YOUR ADDICTION AND THE DEADLY NIGHT OF YOUR DELIVERANCE. HIS FEW DEMONS THAT REMAIN WITHIN THEIR ADDICTIONS, HE'S GOING TO DISCHARGE THEM, FOR YOU HAVE BEEN DELIVERED!

THERE ARE MANY OF YOU

SATAN KNOWS YOU, BUT THERE ARE MANY OF YOU AND YOU ARE NOT THE ONLY YOU! GOD IS DESTROYING HIS DEMONS IN THEIR DRUG ADDICTIONS BECAUSE THE SERPENT IS NO LONGER IN THE DEVIL'S HORN. SATAN KNOWS HE HAS TORMENTED YOU WITH GREAT FEAR. YET, YOU ARE STILL ALIVE! HE HAS DECEIVED YOU WITH HIGH POTENCY DRUGS. YET, YOU ARE STILL ALIVE! HE HAS ENTICED YOU WITH THE NAKED FRUITS OF DEADLY PLEASURES AND NEARLY SCARED YOUR FRIGHTENED LITTLE SOUL TO DEATH! YET, YOU ARE STILL ALIVE. GOD DELIVERED YOU FROM IT ALL AND YET YOU ARE STILL ALIVE! THANKS BE TO YOU, LORD, FOR THY DELIVERANCE. WHEN USING GOD'S WORDS THE DEMONS SET YOU FREE BY THE WORD OF GOD THAT BE IN THEE. SATAN IN ALL HIS DECEPTIONS NOW SEES YOU DO GOOD WHEN AT ONE TIME YOU DID EVIL.

DEMON FEAR GOD MORE THAN YOU

HIS DEMONS WHICH FEAR AND TREMBLE (James 2:19) AT THE THUNDEROUS WORD OF GOD WILL ASK THEIR DADDY WHY THEY SHOULD REMAIN IN THEIR ADDICTION SINCE YOU HAVE BECOME GODLY IN ALL YOUR WAYS. THESE DEVILS FEAR GOD MORE THAN YOU, BUT NOW THEY KNOW EXACTLY WHAT YOU WILL DO. YES LORD, THEY KNOW AS SOON AS YOU FEEL THE EFFECTS OF THE DRUGS, THE SUDDEN FEAR OF THE DEVIL WILL COME UPON YOU, YOU WLL GET SCARED, IMMEDIATELY CALL ON THE LORD, AND GOD'S WORDS WILL DELIVER YOU WHILE DESTROYING THEM (Mark 16:17). THEY KNOW THE WORD OF GOD IS IN YOU AND NOW THEY ARE AFRAID TO ENTER THE ADDICTION BECAUSE YOU ARE COVERED BY THE BLOOD OF THE LAMB. YOU ARE BEING DELIVERED BY GOD FROM THE DEMONS OF THEIR ADDICTION (Matthew 11:28-30)(Revelation 22:17)! HALLELUJAH! THESE DEMONS NEED PERMISSION FROM GOD TO LEAVE THEIR OWN ADDICTION BECAUSE THEY HAVE MET THEIR FATE (Job 2:6). YOUR ADDICTION TO DRUGS IS DESTROYING THEM, BUT DELIVERING YOU. GOOD GOD ALMIGHTY! GOD IS ALMIGHTY!

DO THE OPPOSITE OF YOU

HOW DO YOU STOP USING DRUGS? DO THE OPPOSITE OF HOW YOU STARTED USING DRUGS. YOU STARTED USING DRUGS A CERTAIN WAY, SO YOU STOP USING DRUGS BY DOING THE OPPOSITE WAY OF HOW YOU STARTED. YOU STARTED USING DRUGS BY PUTTING DRUGS ON THE PIPE, SO YOU WILL STOP USING DRUGS BY NOT PUTTING DRUGS ON THE PIPE. HOW SIMPLE CAN YOUR ADDICTION GET? (Corinthians 1:26-27)YOUR ADDICTION IS THE METHOD, NOT SO MUCH AS THE DRUGS ITSELF. WHY ARE YOU MAKING THIS A COMPLICATED THING? WHY ARE YOU STILL PUTTING DRUGS ON THE PIPE? TRY IT AND SEE. STOP BEING SO DOUBTFUL WHEN YOU ARE STILL HITTING THE DEVIL'S HORN. WHATEVER YOUR ADDICTION, IT IS THE METHOD AND PROCESS THAT KEEPS

YOU ADDICTED TO THE ADDICTION. UNDERSTAND YOU! WHEN YOU FIRST STARTED USING DRUGS, DRUGS WERE NOT A PROBLEM TO YOU. YET, ONLY WHEN YOU ALLOWED DRUGS TO USE YOU, DID DRUGS BECOME A PROBLEM TO YOU. THEREFORE, BY CHANGING THE METHOD OF HOW YOU USE DRUGS, GOD WILL DELIVER YOU THROUGH YOUR TRYING EFFORTS AND YOUR SINCERE DESIRES TO STOP USING DRUGS. YOU CAN NOT STOP USING DRUGS ON YOUR OWN BECAUSE DRUGS ARE EVIL, WICKED, AND DEMONIC, BUT WHEN YOU TRY TO STOP USING DRUGS, GOD WILL GIVE YOU THE STRENGTH TO ENDURE (1 Corinthians 10: 13).

LET GOD DRIVE

DO YOU REMEMBER THE VERY FIRST TIME YOU DROVE A CAR? REMEMBER HOW UNSURE YOU WERE? BOTH HANDS ON THE STEERING WHEEL, BOTH FEET ON THE PEDALS AND YOU WERE NERVOUS? THAT WAS THE FIRST TIME YOU EVER DROVE A CAR AND THE ONLY TIME YOU EVER DROVE A CAR. THEN AFTERWARDS IT BECAME AUTOMATIC. NOW YOU DRIVE WITH ONE HAND, ONE FOOT IS WORKING BOTH PEDALS, AND YOU'RE NOT NERVOUS. WHY? BECAUSE SOMETHING WITHIN YOU HAS TAKEN OVER. DRUG ADDICTION HAS THE SAME CONCEPT, BUT IT IS DEMONIC. WHEN THE DEMON TAKES OVER HE WILL DRIVE YOU TO HELL. GOD ALREADY KNOWS THAT DRUGS HAVE TAKEN OVER YOUR LIFE AND YOUR DEMONIC ADDICTION HAS BECOME A PROBLEM TO YOU. HE ALREADY KNOWS THAT YOU ARE TIRED OF USING DRUGS, BUT YOU DO NOT KNOW WHAT KEPT YOU ADDICTED TO DRUGS. HE ALSO KNOWS IF YOU ARE TRULY SERIOUS ABOUT NOT USING DRUGS. IF SO, THIS WOULD BE A GOOD START FOR A NEW DRIVER AND BY CHANGING YOUR METHOD OF HOW YOU USE DRUGS, YOU WILL HAVE SHOWN GOD THAT YOU ARE SUFFERING FROM YOUR DEMONIC ADDICTION AND WANT TO STOP USING DRUGS. YOU WOULD HAVE SHOWN GOD THAT YOU ARE HELPLESS TO DRUGS, AND GOD SAID IF YOU TAKE THE FIRST STEP, HE WILL GIVE YOU THE NEXT TWO. YOU TOOK THE FIRST STEP BY CHANGING THE

METHOD OF HOW YOU USE DRUGS, THEREFORE, GOD WILL TAKE THE NEXT TWO: THE TASTE OF DRUGS OUT OF YOUR MOUTH AND THE CRAVING FOR DRUGS OUT OF YOUR MIND.

THE HOLLOW REED

GOD KNOWS IT TAKES THE ELEMENT OF FIRE TO COOK, USE, AND PROCESS DRUGS. WHAT YOU DO NOT KNOW IS THAT THE FIRE YOU USE IS LIT WITH HELL'S FIRE. THE DRUGS YOU INHALE ARE THE EVIL, WICKED, AND SEDUCTIVE SPIRITS OF THE DEVIL THAT TRANSFORM INTO YOU THROUGH THE SMOKE OF HELL'S FIRE. NOW YOU KNOW THAT THE SERPENT IS A RED HOT PIPE LIT FROM HELL! WHAT KIND OF DEMON DO YOU THINK WAS INSIDE OF YOU? A PIPE DEMON AND HE'S WAITING ON HIS HIT RIGHT NOW, BUT DON'T GIVE INTO THE PIPE DEMON'S DEMANDS. HE'LL DESTROY YOU. DO YOU NOT SEE THE SERPENT IN THE DEVIL'S HORN? YOU GOT TO KNOW WHAT BIT YOU AND A PIPE DEMON IS WHAT BIT YOU (Numbers 21:6)! THERE IS A CURE MADE BY MAN FOR A SNAKE BITE, BUT ONLY GOD CAN CURE YOU FROM A PIPE BITE. YOU HAVE BEEN BITTEN BY THE SERPENT IN THE PIPE. THE PIPE-BITING DEMON HAS BEEN THERE ALL THE TIME HIDING WITHIN YOUR ADDICTION, TO AN ADDICTION, BUT NOW THE SERPENT MUST GO!

THE BLOOD OF THE CROSS

THUS, SAITH THE LORD! BY THE BLOOD OF THE CROSS AND POWER OF THE HOLY GHOST! THE LORD COMMANDS YOU, PIPE DEMON, AND SUFFER YOU NOT A WORD, BUT BE CAST BACK INTO THE ABOMINABLE LAKE OF FIRE FROM WHICH YOU HAVE CAME! FOR AS A VAPOR OF SMOKE YOU RISE AS A DRUG-USING, VENOMOUS SERPENT OUT OF HELL AND THROUGH THE "HOLLOW REED OF AN IRON ROD," YOU HAVE DECEIVED THE GENTILES THEREOF (Revelation 11:1) THUS, AS A CURSED TEMPLE OUT OF COURT. FROM THIS DAY FORTH, THOU SHALL

BE MANIFESTED IN THE FLESH. THAT ALL WHO READ, SEE, AND UNDERSTAND THEIR DEMONIC ADDICTION UNTO YOU SHALL BE NO MORE. THUS, SAITH THE LORD! YOU MUST MEASURE THE TEMPLE OF GOD BY YOUR FAITH THROUGH THE HOLLOW REED OF YOUR IRON CLAD ADDICTION AND YOU MUST COME UNTO THE ALTAR OF GOD AND WORSHIP HIM. GOD WILL DELIVER YOU FROM THE SERPENT IN THE DEVIL'S HORN. THUS, SAITH THE LORD! PUT GOD FIRST IN WHATEVER YOU DO AND YOUR ADDICTION WILL FLEE FROM YOU JUST LIKE THE DEVIL.

PROCESS OF AN ADDICTION

HOW DO YOU STOP USING DRUGS? YOU MUST UNDERSTAND THE PROCESS YOU GO THROUGH BEFORE YOU USE DRUGS. THE HOUSE IS CLEAN. THE CHILDREN ARE OVER TO THEIR GRANDMOTHER'S HOUSE, AND NOW IT IS TIME TO RELAX AND TAKE A BIG HIT! IS THIS YOUR PROCESS? DO YOU LIKE MAKING SURE THE COAST IS CLEAR BEFORE YOU USE DRUGS? DO YOU LIKE USING DRUGS ONLY IN THE BATHROOM, GARAGE, OR ON YOUR BACK PORCH? WHAT ABOUT IN CLUBS, CARS, OR OVER YOUR BEST FRIEND'S HOUSE? DO YOU KNOW YOUR FAVORITE PLACE WHERE YOU USE DRUGS ARE PART OF THE PROCESS THAT KEEPS YOU ADDICTED TO DRUGS? YOU SHOULD KNOW THIS FROM GOING BACK AND FORTH TO THE SAME PLACE EVERY TIME YOU USE DRUGS. DO YOU LIKE TAKING A HIT WHILE STANDING OUTSIDE IN THE DARK AND LOOKING IN EVERY DIRECTION? FOR WHAT, AND FOR WHO? YOU ARE LOOKING FOR YOU AND THE PROCESSES THAT YOU GO THROUGH BEFORE YOU USE DRUGS ARE KILLING YOU. ARE YOU AWARE OF ALL THE HUSTLING, BEGGING, BORROWING, AND STEALING YOU DO BEFORE YOU USE DRUGS? THESE ARE THE PROCESSES THAT KEEP YOU ADDICTED TO DRUGS. THUS, STOP HUSTLING FOR DRUGS!

TALKING TO ANOTHER YOU

UNDERSTAND YOU! IF THE ONLY THING YOU KNOW ABOUT DRUGS WOULD BE TO USE DRUGS THEN YOU KNOW VERY LITTLE ABOUT DRUGS. WHAT DO YOU KNOW ABOUT DRUGS OTHER THAN GETTING HIGH, MASTERBATING, OR FINDING SOME WOMEN TO FREAK? WOE! LET US KEEP IT REAL WITH YOU. THIS MAY BE YOUR LAST TIME TALKING TO ANOTHER YOU. THE DEMONS OF YOUR ADDICTION ARE ALREADY FIENDING FOR ANOTHER HIT, BUT BEFORE YOU TAKE THAT HIT, REMEMBER, YOU ARE A MASTER BLASTER AND A WALKING DISASTER . ONCE SPRUNG, YOU TAKE OFF RUNNING OUT OF FEAR. YOU HAVE COTTON MOUTH WHEN YOU GET BACK AND THEN YOU STAND AROUND LOOKING SCARED AND STUPID! EVERYBODY KNOWS YOU ARE ON DRUGS. YOU HARDLY EAT, RARELY SLEEP, AND ARE ALWAYS BROKE. WOE! WHY DON'T YOU GET YOUR HAIR CUT WITH THAT MONEY INSTEAD OF A HIT? YOU LOOK LIKE AN OVERGROWN YARD THAT NEEDS WEEDING. FOR YOU ARE NOT A DRUG ADDICT, NOR ARE YOU ADDICTED TO DRUGS! YET, YOU LOOK AT YOU EVERY DAY, AND YOU STILL DO NOT SEE WHAT IS WRONG WITH YOU? DO YOU NOT SEE YOU? A PAIR OF PANTS, A CLEAN SHIRT, AND A DECENT PAIR OF SHOES FROM A YARD SALE IS LESS THAN A $10.00 HIT, BUT DRUGS HAVE YOU SO UNCARING ABOUT YOU. YOU ARE AWAYS RAGGEDY, DIRTY, AND WEARING THE SAME FILTHY CLOTHING. NOBODY HAS TO TELL YOU ABOUT YOU, THUS, YOU KNOW YOU! FOR YOU ARE THE BLACK SHEEP. DO YOU NOT SEE YOUR WOOL IS OFF AND THE BODY HAS BEEN EXPOSED NAKED? WHO IS GOING TO BE NICE TO YOU WHEN YOU HAVE NO SHAME? THUS, GET OFF YOUR PITY POT YOU! NO ONE CARES ABOUT YOUR DEMONS FIENDING FOR DRUGS, BUT YOU!

TAKE CARE OF YOU

HOW TO STOP USING DRUGS? YOU MUST TAKE CARE OF YOU AS YOU DO WHAT YOU DO AND GOD WILL DELIVER YOU. WHAT HAPPENED TO THE PRIDE YOU ONCE HELD SO HIGH? IT IS GOOD TO BE HUMBLE, BUT NOT LAZY. YOU HOP AROUND LIKE

A GRASSHOPPER ALL DAY AND YOU ONLY LOOK FOR ENOUGH WORK TO GET ANOTHER PIECE OF DOPE. IN PLAIN WORDS, ADAM, BE A MAN AND, EVE, SLOW DOWN. YOU CAN NOT HIT THEM ALL. YOU HAVE TO MISS A FEW AND GET SOME SLEEP! YOUR FAMILY LIFE, SOCIAL LIFE, POLITICAL LIFE, PHYSICAL LIFE, AND YOUR SPIRITUAL LIFE ARE A PART OF YOU.THESE ARE THE THINGS OF YOU THAT SHOULD BE DONE AND NOT ONE OF THEM BY YOU SHOULD BE LEFT UNDONE. YOU HAVE SHIRKED YOUR RESPONSIBILITY LONG ENOUGH. FOR YOU HAVE ALLOWED DRUGS TO DESTROY THE WORKS OF YOUR HANDS, DREAMS OF YOUR FUTURE, AND YOUR THOUGHTS OF TOMORROW.

KNOW ABOUT DRUGS

HOW DO YOU STOP USING DRUGS? KNOW ABOUT DRUGS! DO YOU KNOW WHAT DRUGS YOU ARE ADDICTED TO? ARE YOU AWARE THAT THE COCAINE YOU SHOOT, SNORT, AND SMOKE DERIVED FROM A PLANT MADE BY GOD; IT PROCESSED BY MAN. YOU SHOULD ALSO KNOW HEROIN IS A PLANT MADE BY GOD, DERIVED OUT OF A GOVERNMENTAL FUNDED LAB PROCESSED BY MAN. WISDOM TEACHES THAT CERTAIN PLANTS WERE PUT HERE BY GOD TO BE USED FOR MANY PURPOSES. PERHAPS, MEDICAL REASONING, BUT EVEN YOU SHOULD KNOW THAT ANY LABORATORY DRUG PROCESSED BY MAN, IS NOT OF GOD. EVERY PLANT PLANTED BY GOD IS UNTOUCHED BY MAN AND IT IS OF GOD, BUT WHEN MAN MANIPULATES ITS GROWTH AND BREAKS DOWN THE MOLECULAR STRUCTURES OF THE PLANT, IT IS THEN POLLUTED AND IS NO LONGER OF GOD. MAN HAS MUTATED THE PLANT FROM ITS NATURAL GROWTH, THUS IT TURNS INTO A SOLID, LIQUID, OR GAS DEVIL BECAUSE IT IS DEMONIC.

KNOWLEDGE OF DRUGS

DURING THE BUILDING OF THE RAILROAD, MIGRANT CHINESE PEOPLE WERE THE MAIN LABORERS. THEY BROUGHT WITH

THEM FROM THEIR COUNTRY OPIATES. NINETY PERCENT OF THE CHINESE PEOPLE IN THEIR COUNTRY, AT ONE TIME OR ANOTHER, WERE ADDICTED TO OPIATES. THEN, THE PEOPLE IN THE UNITED STATES BECAME ADDICTED TO THE OPIATES. TO COMBAT THEIR ADDICTIONS, THE GOVERNMENT INTRODUCED SOCIETY TO HEROIN BACK WHEN WE DIDN'T HAVE THE USDA FOOD AND DRUG ADMINISTRATION TO DO RESEARCH ON DRUGS. DRUGS AND DRUG ADDICTIONS WERE A FAIRLY NEW THING. SINCE THEN, MILLIONS OF PEOPLE HAVE DIED FROM THEIR HEROIN OVERDOSES AND THOUSANDS ARE STILL DYING FROM THE LABORATORY EXPERIMENTAL DISEASE EVEN TO THIS DAY. THIS CATASTROPHIC DRUG EPIDEMIC IN THE UNITED STATES WAS CONSIDERED A DISEASE BACK THEN. THE GOVERNMENT SOON REALIZED THE SIDE EFFECTS OF HEROIN WERE FAR WORSE THAN THE OPIUM.

JUNKIES OVER NIGHT

PEOPLE BECAME JUNKIES OVERNIGHT. YOU COULD SEE THEM STANDING IN BUNCHES AND GROVES, SITTING ON STREET CORNERS, HANGING IN DOORWAYS, AND LAYING OUT ON FRONT LAWNS NODDING WITH NEEDLES DANGLING FROM THEIR ARMPITS. THOSE WHO COULD NOT AFFORD THEIR FIX WERE SICK, VOMITING, CRAMPING, SCRATCHING, AND BENDING OVER IN SEVERE PAIN AS IF THEY WERE DYING. THE GOVERNMENT HURRIED UP AND OUTLAWED THEIR DOPE AND SEVERELY PUNISHED ANYONE CAUGHT USING OR DISTRIBUTING HEROIN AS IT IS UNTO THIS DAY. PERHAPS, BACK THEN, HEROIN ADDICTION HELPED SPEARHEAD THE CONTROL SUBSTANCE LAW BECAUSE JUNKIES WOULD LITERALLY KILL YOU FOR A FEW PENNIES IN ORDER TO ESCAPE AND AVOID THE SICKNESS THAT CAME FROM THEIR HEROINIC ADDICTION. THE GOVERNMENT INTRODUCED HEROIN TO SOCIETY AND PRODUCED THE WORST AND STRONGEST TRADEMARK DRUG OF ALL DRUGS OF ITS KIND. TO THIS DAY, JUNKIES ARE STILL DYING FROM THE NEEDLES AND HANGING ON TO THE VEINS OF THEIR LIVES. YET, NO ONE IS

TO BE BLAMED FOR THEIR SUFFERINGS. NO ONE IS TO BE BLAMED FOR THEIR SORROWS, THEIR SICKNESS, THEIR MISERIES, AND THEIR ADDICTIONS. NOPE! NOT ONE PERSON IS TO BE BLAMED FOR THEIR DEATH – NOT EVEN THE GOVERNMENT WHICH PROFITS FROM DRUGS.

PROBABILITY OF LIFE

HOW DO YOU STOP USING DRUG? KEEP IN MIND YOU ARE NOT ADDICTED TO A DRUG UNTIL YOU USE THE DRUG. THEREFORE, UNTIL YOU ALLOW YOURSELF TO USE DRUGS, YOU ARE NOT ADDICTED TO DRUGS. THE DEVIL WANTS YOU TO ENJOY THE WONDERFUL FEELING YOU THINK YOU GET WHEN YOU USE DRUGS AND HE WANTS YOU TO KEEP THINKING YOU ARE ADDICTED TO DRUGS. HE KNOWS YOU DON'T EVEN HAVE A CLUE, NOR HAS IT EVER OCCURED TO YOU THAT WHEN YOU USE DRUGS, YOU DO NOT HAVE LONG TO LIVE. THE LAW OF SCIENCE ASSURES SATAN THAT YOU ARE GOING TO GET CAUGHT GETTING HIGH AT LEAST ONE TIME. THERE IS NO RIGHT WAY TO GET HIGH, BUT THERE IS A WRONG WAY TO USE DRUGS. THE RIGHT WAY TO GET HIGH WITH THE DEVIL IS THE WRONG DRUG FOR YOU. THE LAW OF PROBABILITY IS EVERYTHING IS 50/50. IN OTHER WORDS, YOU ARE PROBABLY FIFTY PERCENT GOOD AND FIFTY PERCENT EVIL, BUT ON THE SCALE OF LIFE, YOU TIP BACK AND FORTH. WHEN YOU USE DRUGS, DOES YOUR RIGHT OUTWEIGH YOUR WRONG? HOW CAN YOU EXPECT TO GET OFF OF DRUGS WHEN YOU ARE A DEVIL ON DRUGS?! THE DEVIL IS A LIE AND THE FATHER OF A LIE. DO DRUGS MAKE YOU A LIAR? THE DEVIL HAS NO POWER OVER YOU UNTIL YOU SUBMIT TO HIS WILL. DO YOU SUBMIT TO SATAN'S WILL?

RESIST SATAN

THE BIBLE SAYS RESIST SATAN AND HE WILL FLEE FROM YOU (James 4:7). DO YOU COMMAND SATAN TO FLEE FROM YOU IN CHRIST'S NAME? NO! YOU PREFER THE DEVIL TO BE IN YOU BY

USING DRUGS. WHAT? YOU ARE YOUR WORST ENEMY, FOR YOU ARE LIKE A MAN BEGGING FOR A CIGARETTE AT THE TOBACCO STORE. FIRST, HE IS IN THE WRONG PLACE BEGGING BECAUSE THEY SELL THEM INSIDE THE STORE, BUT SINCE DRUGS HAVE TAKEN HIS MONEY, IN HIS MIND HE IS IN THE RIGHT PLACE. SURELY, SOMEBODY WILL GIVE HIM A CIGARETTE OUT OF TWENTY AND HIS ODDS OF GETTING ONE ARE MUCH GREATER WHERE THEY ARE BEING SOLD THAN IT WOULD BE WALKING THE BACK STREETS. YOU THINK YOU ARE PLAYING IT SAFE, BUT EVERY HIT YOU TAKE IS LIKE A NIGHTMARE AND YOUR HIGH BECOMES THE EPITOME OF HELL! WOE! SATAN PUT ANOTHER NAIL IN YOUR COFFIN AND HE'S BOXING YOU IN FOR THAT ULTIMATE HIT (death). THAT IS WHY YOU SENSE DEATH EVERY TIME YOU GET HIGH, FOR YOU ALREADY KNOW YOU ARE DYING. WOE! YOU BECOME AS NERVOUS AS A REFORMED CRACKHEAD WOMAN IN CHURCH. AT LEAST SHE KNOWS SHE HAS PROSTITUTED HERSELF IN HER ADDICTION AND HAS REPENTED WHOLE-HEARTEDLY TO GOD THAT HE FORGIVE HER SINS, BUT NOT YOU! YOU ACT AS IF YOU HAVE DONE NO WRONG! NO ONE CAN TELL YOU ANYTHING AND YOU KNOW EVERYTHING! YET, YOU KNOW NOTHING ABOUT YOU! DO YOU KNOW YOU KNOW YOU?

DO YOU KNOW YOU KNOW YOU?

WHY DID YOU LIE DOWN WITH THAT MAN? WOE! DO YOU KNOW YOU KNOW YOU? THEN WHY DID YOU SEDUCE THE MOTHER AND HER DAUGHTER? WOE! DO YOU KNOW YOU KNOW YOU? WHAT IS IN YOUR ADDICTION THAT YOU WON'T DO OR HAVE NOT ALREADY DONE FOR DRUGS? WHY DID YOU LOOK AT THAT INNOCENT, YOUNG GIRL WITH LUST IN YOUR EYES? WHY DID YOU SNEAK BACK OVER TO YOUR BEST FRIEND'S HOUSE TO BE WITH HIS WIFE? WHY DO YOU LIE ABOUT THINGS YOU DO AND WHAT MAKES YOU THINK YOU KNOW YOU? DO YOU THINK YOU KNOW YOU BY WHAT YOU DO? THUS, DO YOU THINK WHAT YOU DO WAS DONE BY YOU? YOU SAY YOU KNOW YOU, BUT KNOW YOU NOT THAT WHAT

YOU DO, WAS NOT YOU NOR WAS IT DONE BY YOU! UNDERSTAND YOU! WHATEVER YOU DO IN YOUR ADDICTION WAS NOT YOU, BUT THE SIN OF GOD THAT DWELLS IN YOU (Philippians 2:13). THEREFORE, HOW CAN YOU STOP USING DRUGS NOT KNOWING YOU NEED JESUS CHRIST IN YOUR ADDICTIVE LIFE TO DELIVER YOU FROM THE SINS OF YOUR ADDICTION? YOU ARE NOT THE SIN OF GOD THAT DWELLS IN YOUR ADDICTION, BUT YOUR ADDICTION IS THE SIN OF GOD THAT DWELLS IN YOU AND ONLY CHRIST CAN DELIVER YOU FROM SUCH SINS. YOU WERE BORN IN SIN AND SHAPED IN INIQUITY AND IT IS THE SIN OF GOD THAT DWELLS IN YOU THAT HELPS YOU FIND THE LORD THROUGH THE THINGS YOU DO. IT IS YOUR ADDICTION THAT MAKES YOU DO WHAT YOU DO AND GO THROUGH WHAT YOU GO THROUGH IN ORDER FOR YOU TO FIND THE GOD IN YOU. (Psalm 51:5)YOU ARE YOU AREN'T YOU? YET, YOUR ADDICTION IS THE SIN OF YOU IN ALL SHAPES, FORMS, AND FASHIONS.

DO YOU CONDEMN YOU?

WHO ELSE CAN JUDGE YOU BY WHAT YOU DO OTHER THAN GOD? DO YOU CONDEMN YOU FOR WHAT YOU DO? NEITHER DOES THE GOD IN YOU. THEREFORE, HOW CAN YOU STOP USING DRUGS CONDEMING EVERYTHING YOU DO YET, UNAWARE THAT IT WAS THE SIN OF GOD THAT DWELLS IN YOU? FOR IF YOU REALLY KNEW YOU, YOU WOULD KNOW THAT YOU ARE AT A DEAD LEVEL AND UNLESS SOMEONE CAN CONFER UPON YOU 90 DEGREE KNOWLEDGE OF YOUR SINFUL DRUG ADDICTION, YOU WILL DIE. YOU HAVE PLAYED YOUR LAST GAME AND YOU ARE TAKING YOUR LAST HIT! YOU HAVE COME TO THE END OF YOUR ADDICTION AND YOU CAN NOT CON GOD! DO YOU WANT TO LIVE OR DO YOU WANT TO DIE? DO YOU WANT TO STAY AT A DEAD LEVEL OR DO YOU WANT TO RISE ABOVE YOUR ADDICTION AND BECOME A LIVING PERPENDICULAR? YOU MUST BE RESURRECTED BY GOD FROM A DEAD LEVEL AND BECOME UPRIGHT ABOUT YOUR EVERYTHING. THAT IS HOW YOU STOP USING DRUGS!

TO KNOW GOOD AND EVIL

"BEHOLD, THE MAN HAS BECOME AS ONE OF US, TO KNOW GOOD AND EVIL. AND NOW, LEST HE PUT FORTH HIS HAND, AND TAKE ALSO OF THE TREE OF LIFE, AND EAT, AND LIVE FOREVER" (Genesis 3:22). GOD CREATED YOU NOT FOR WHAT YOU DO, BUT TO KNOW HIM THROUGH WHAT YOU DO AND BY THE SINS OF YOU. DO YOU NOT KNOW THAT GOD DWELLS IN YOU? GOD GAVE YOU A CONSCIOUS TO KNOW WHEN YOU HAVE BEEN GOOD AND TO KNOW WHEN YOU HAVE BEEN EVIL. YOU KNOW WHEN YOU WERE RIGHT AND YOU KNOW WHEN YOU WERE WRONG. MY GOODNESS, ADAM, STOP MAKING EXCUSES FOR YOURSELF EVE! GET OFF YOUR KNEES, STAND UP, AND START BEING A MAN! SPEAK TO THESE DRY BONES IN THE VALLEY (Ezekiel 37:1-14)! CRY OUT UNTO THE GOD OF THY SALVATION (Isaiah 17:10) CALL ON THE LORD! HE WILL DELIVER YOU. BUT, WHAT ABOUT YOU, MY SISTER? WILL YOU NOT SEEK THE LORD? GOD WORKS WITH YOUR EFFORTS, NOT YOUR SLOTHFULNESS! HE WORKS WITH YOUR ENDURANCE IN ALL THINGS (Romans 15:5-6). GOD KNOWS WHAT YOU NEED BEFORE YOU EVEN ASK HIM FOR WHAT YOU NEED. YOU MUST BECOME RIGHTEOUS ENOUGH IN YOUR WAYS TO RECEIVE FROM GOD WHAT YOU NEED. GOD GIVES TO EACH MAN ACCORDING TO HIS OWN DEEDS (Romans 2:6) AND HE JUDGES ALL SIN ON THE SAME MERITS. HE DIDN'T BRING YOU THIS FAR TO LEAVE YOU NOW. YOU USE AT LEAST $50.00 DOLLARS PER DAY ON DOPE. MULTIPLY THAT BY SEVEN DAYS A WEEK WHICH IS $350.00 PER WEEK. MULTIPLY THAT BY FOUR WEEKS WHICH AVERAGES $1,400.00 PER MONTH. WOE!

SATAN'S LITTLE IMPS

SATAN'S DRUG DEALING LITTLE IMPS WILL ROB YOU FOR OVER HALF OF YOUR CHECK EACH MONTH AND NOW YOU WONDER WHY YOU MARE ALWAYS RAGGEDY, SMELL BAD, AND ARE BROKE. WOE! YOU WONDER WHY YOU DO NOT HAVE ANYTHING OF VALUE AND WHERE ALL YOUR MONEY GOD GAVE

YOU WENT? YOU KNOW EXACTLY WHAT YOU DID WITH IT AND EVERYONE ELSE KNOWS WHAT YOU DID WITH IT, SO THERE IS NO SECRET ABOUT IT. IT IS OBVIOUS TO YOU AND EVERYONE WHO KNOWS YOU, THAT YOU USE DRUGS. EVERYTHING ABOUT YOU IS IN THE OPEN EXCEPT YOUR ADDICTION THAT YOU TRY TO HIDE IN THE DARK. YOU LIVE IN FEAR, YOU FACE DAMNATION, AND YOU ARE NEAR DEATH. YOUR SOUL IS DYING, BUT BY THE POWER OF GOD, WRETCHED MAN, AND THE RIGHTEOUSNESS OF CHRIST, HE IS IN YOU.

THE DAY THE LORD HAS MADE

YOU ARE DELIVERED FROM YOUR DRUGGAFIED STATE OF MIND. YOU HAVE COMMITTED AN ABOMINATION WORTHY OF DEATH, BUT BY THE SELF-RIGHTEOUSNES OF YOU, BLACK SHEEP, YOU ARE NO LONGER AT A DEAD LEVEL. THEREFORE, STAND, AND RISE, MAN AND WOMAN OF GOD, AND BELIEVE IN THE HOLY POWERS OF THE LORD THAT IS WITHIN YOU (1 John 4: 4).THIS IS THE DAY THAT THE LORD HAS MADE. THEREFORE, LET US REJOICE AND BE GLAD IN IT (Psalm 118:24). GOD HAS GIVEN YOU KNOWLEDGE OF YOUR ADDICTION TO NO DEGREE AND IN YOUR SUFFERING HAS THE LORD DECLARED YOUR DELIVERANCE. "ASK OF ME SAITH THE LORD, AND I WILL GIVE UNTO THEE THE HEATHEN FOR THY INHERITANCE, AND THE UTTERMOST PARTS OF THE EARTH FOR THY POSSESSION" (Psalm 2:8). GOD HAS GRACED YOU WITH UNLIMITED KNOWLEDGE OF YOUR ADDICTION AND YOU CAN SEE THE DEVIL COMING BEFORE HE EVEN GEST TO YOU. DRUGS HAVE NO POWER OVER YOU IN YOUR DELIVERANCE! HALLELUJAH! HE IS A GOOD GOD AND HE EXPECTS FOR YOU TO BECOME MORE RIGHTEOUS IN YOUR DAILY DEALINGS AT ALL TIMES AND IN ALL THINGS. IN OTHER WORDS, TRY TO DO THE RIGHT THING SOMETIMES, IF NOT ALWAYS. UNDERSTAND YOU! GOD WILL DELIVER YOU THROUGH THE RIGHTEOUSNESS OF YOU AND BY YOUR TRYING EFFORTS TO STOP USING DRUGS.

MYSTERY OF YOU

THE MYSTERY OF WHO YOU ARE AS A BLACK SHEEP IS YOUR UNRIGHTEOUSNESS TO GOD. ALL YOUR LIFE YOU HAVE BEEN A VERY HARD-HEADED BLACK SHEEP. YOU KNOW THIS, BUT YOU JUST HAD TO EXPERIENCE THIS WAY OF LIFE FOR YOURSELF. YOU WOULD NOT LISTEN TO YOUR MOTHER WHEN SHE WARNED YOU ABOUT THE WHOLE WORLD GOD PLACED IN YOUR HEART (Job 11:13-20). UNLIKE YOUR BROTHERS AND SISTERS WHO STAYED BY THE SHEPHERD TENT, YOU JUST HAD TO SEE FOR YOURSELF OTHERWISE, YOU WOULD NOT BE THE BLACK SHEEP. NOW, MY LITTLE SHEEP, YOU ARE LOST FROM THE FATHER AND SEPERATED FROM THE GOSPEL OF JESUS CHRIST. YOU ARE DEMONICALLY ADDICTED TO A DRUG THAT HAS DESTROYED THE BONDS BETWEEN YOU, FAMILY, AND FRIENDS. THUS, YOU HAVE LEARNED THE WAYS OF THE WICKED WORLD AND NOW YOU ARE CAUGHT UP IN THE CRACKS AND CREVICES OF YOUR SINFUL LIFE EXPERIENCES. THE END THEREOF YOU DID NOT SEE WHICH LED TO DRUGS. A DEMONIC ADDICTION YOU SUFFERS MUCH GREATER THAN YOU, BUT BY THE RIGHTEOUNESS OF YOU, BLACK SHEEP, YOU WILL OVERCOME YOUR ADDICTION, BUT ONLY THROUGH OUR LORD AND SAVIOR CHRIST JESUS. AS SURE AS THERE IS A DIFFERENCE BETWEEN A CRACKHEAD AND A CRACK SMOKER, BLACK SHEEP, THERE IS A DIFFERENCE BETWEEN YOU AND THE REST OF YOUR FAMILY.

THE ANOINTED ONE

YOU ARE THE ONE, BLACK SHEEP. THE ONE GOD HAS CHOSEN OUT OF THE ENTIRE FAMILY TO MAKE THE WHOLE. YOU ARE THE ONE GOD HAS CHOSEN TO DO HIS WILL, SPREAD HIS GOSPEL, AND FURTHER HIS KINGDOM. IT IS YOU, THE ANOINTED ONE OF GOD. YET, YOU ARE UNAWARE THAT YOU ARE THE YOU. YOU HAVE SHIRKED YOUR RESPONSIBILITY AND YOU HAVE REFUSED GOD'S INSTRUCTIONS, BUT THE FAMILY DEPENDED ON YOU TO DO THE RIGHT THING IN YOUR

ADDICTION. THEY ALL KNOW GOD CHOSE YOU TO BE HIS DISCIPLE, BUT LOOK AT YOU! YOU ARE UNAWARE THAT YOU ARE THE YOU! THUS, YOU SHOULD KNOW YOU ARE THE YOU FROM HOW THE FAMILY CRADLES TO YOU! YOU SHOULD KNOW THAT YOU ARE THE YOU FROM HOW THEY VALUE YOUR OPINIONS. FOR YOU SHOULD KNOW YOU ARE THE YOU, BLACK SHEEP, FROM HOW THEY RESPECTED YOU, LOOKED UP TO YOU, AND DEPENDED ON YOU. THIS SHOULD TELL YOU THAT YOU ARE THE YOU.

FOR NOW, THEY TALK ABOUT YOU, BLACK SHEEP. AND THEY WATCH YOU. THEY ARE DISAPPOINTED IN YOU BECAUSE GOD CHOSE YOU TO BE THE YOU, BUT LOOK AT YOU! DO YOU NOT SEE THE GOD IN YOU? GOD CHOSE YOU ABOVE ALL THE REST, BUT WHAT HAVE YOU DONE FOR THE REST EXCEPT GOTTEN OTHER FAMILY MEMBERS HOOKED ON DRUGS? WOE! YOU HAVE CAUSED YOUR OWN BROTHERS AND SISTERS TO STUMBLE (1 Corinthians 8: 9-13) (1 Timothy 4: 12). YET, GOD FORGIVES YOU, BUT IN YOUR ADDICTION THEY ARE RIGHT ABOUT YOU. YOU ARE NOT THE SAME YOU. THUS, BLACK SHEEP, YOU ARE YOU, BUT WHEN YOU USE DRUGS YOU ARE NO LONGER YOU. YOUR ADDICTION MAKES YOU SOMEONE OTHER THAN YOU, BUT WHO? ARE YOU NOT THE YOU, FOR YOU ACT AS IF YOU HAVE DONE NO WRONG AND AS IF YOU DON NOT EVEN CARE. WHAT IS WRONG WITH YOU? DO YOU NOT KNOW YOU ARE THE YOU?

JOSEPH, ARE YOU!

YOU MUST UNDERSTAND THE STORY OF JOSEPH IS GOD'S PURPOSE FOR YOU (Genesis 37:1-50). GOD PUT HIM THROUGH WHAT HE WENT THROUGH, AS HE HAS YOU, IN ORDER FOR HIM TO SAVE HIS FAMILY, BUT WHO CAN SAVE YOU FROM YOU? WILL YOU NOT SEEK THE GOD IN YOU? WHO KNOWS HOW LONG IT WILL TAKE BEFORE THE LORD SENDS ANOTHER YOU TO YOU, BUT REST ASSURED, THE ANGEL OF DEATH WILL COME BEFORE HE DOES. IN THE MEANWHILE, WHO TENDS TO

THE FAMILY MATTERS? CERTAINLY NOT YOU! FORGIVE HIM, MY LORD, HE KNOWS NOT THAT HE KNOWS NOT. THE ANGEL OF DEATH IS UPON HIM AND LIKE A BLACK SHEEP HEADING FOR SLAUGHTER, HE STILL EXPERIMENTS WITH DRUGS.

CRACKHEADS AND CRACK SMOKERS

THE DIFFERENCE BETWEEN A CRACKHEAD AND A CRACK SMOKER IS THEIR USAGE OF DRUGS AND THE KNOWLEDGE THEY HAVE OF THEIR ADDICTIONS. A CRACKHEAD SMOKES AT ALL TIMES AND HE IS NEVER TOO BUSY TO STOP AND TAKE ANOTHER HIT. AS A MATTER OF FACT, HE WANTS A HIT RIGHT NOW AND A MOMENT EARLIER WAS NOT SOON ENOUGH. A CRACKHEAD PIPE STAYS ON FIRE BECAUSE HE LOVES TO SEE THE SMOKE . THUS, LIKE THE CLOUDS OF HEAVEN IN A GLASS BOWL, HELL IS BELOW THE FIRE UNDER HIS PIPE. A CRACKHEAD WILL ROD AND PUSH THAT DAMN THING ALL NIGHT TRYING TO GET THAT LAST HIT. HE WILL TAKE OUT YOUR TRASH, WASH YOUR CAR, MOW YOUR LAWN, AND PAINT YOUR WHOLE HOUSE FOR A GOOD HIT! HE IS WORSE THAN AN ADDICTED WINE-O LYING ON SIDE OF THE LIQUOR STORE PISSY DRUNK. A WINE-O WILL AWAKEN FROM HIS DRUKEN STUPOR AND REALIZE HE HAS PISSED ON HIMSELF. NOT A CRACKHEAD. A CRACKHEAD SEES NO FURTHER THAN HIS PIPES AND WILL PICK UP ANYTHING THAT LOOKS LIKE DRUGS. TO A CRACKHEAD, ANYTHING THAT LOOKS LIKE A ROCK IS A ROCK UNTIL HE MISSES HIS HIT.

TWO THINGS: PIPE AND A LIGHTER

HE IS KNOWN FOR HAVING TWO THINGS ON HIS PERSON AT ALL TIMES: A PIPE AND LIGHTER. NO DRUGS. A LIGHTER IS A VAUABLE THING IN A DRUG ADDICTION, BUT HIS PIPE IS WORTH A HIT. UNFORTUNATELY, MOST CRACKHEADS SUFFER AT THE FATE OF THEIR FAMILY MEMBERS BECAUSE THEIR ADDICTIONS HAVE BURNED THEIR BRIDGES. THEY DO NOT

TRUST THEM IN THEIR HOUSE, NEAR THEIR HOUSE, OR VISITING THEIR HOUSES REGARDLESS OF HOW CLOSELY A FAMILY MEMBER WATCHES THEIR BELONGINGS. WHEN A CRACK HEAD LEAVES, SOMETHING ALWAYS COME UP MISSING. AS A RESULT, MANY CRACKHEADS ARE OFTEN BEATEN, STOMPED, SHOT, CUT, STABBED, AND KILLED ON EVERY STREET CORNER IN A CITY. ONE IS FOUND DEAD IN EACH AND EVERY OTHER NEIGHBORHOOD OF A COMMUNITY. A CRACKHEAD LIVES TO GET HIGH AND HIS MIND IS NEVER TOO FAR FROM HIS NEXT HIT. WHEN HE TAKES THAT HIT, IT IS THE BALL GAME. THE HIGH COMPLETELY TAKE HIS SENSE OF REASONING AND HE IS VOID OF ALL UNDERSTANDING. HE WILL SMOKE, SNORT, SHOOT, TOOT, TASTE, FREAK, AND PARLAY A DRUG DEALER'S DOPE AS IF IT WAS FOR FREE AND THE MONEY HE MAKES OFF A FEW SALES, WILL BE SPENT WITH OTHER DEALERS, INCLUDING HIS OWN.

WHEN THE HIGH IS OVER

THUS, ONCE THE SMOKE HAS CLEARED AND THE HIGH IS OVER, A CRACKHEAD WILL COME TO HIS SENSES AND REALIZE HE HAS SMOKED, FREAKED, AND PARLAYED A KILLER'S DOPE. THE DEADLY DEVIL'S DOPE! NERVOUSLY, HE WILL GO INTO HIDING, BUT NOT BEFORE HE HAS EXHAUSTED ALL HIS POWER THAT NIGHT IN TRYING TO SECURE ONE LAST HIT. OF COURSE, HE IS SNITCHED ON BY OTHER ADDICTS SEARCHING FOR THEIR DEMONS. A CRACKHEAD IS OFTEN FOUND, BUT BEING THAT IT IS THE DEVIL'S DOPE, UNFORTUNATELY, ANOTHER ONE WILL COME UP MISSING.

UNLIKE A CRACKHEAD, A CRACK SMOKER CAN TAKE A HIT AND PASS THE PIPE, AND YOU WILL NEVER KNOW WHEN HE IS HIGH. HE IS NOT A FOOL'S JUNKIE, AND HE DOES NOT LIVE ON THE STREETS. HE KNOWS THE NATURE OF THE DRUGS AND HE IS AWARE OF THE FEAR THAT COMES WITH ITS USAGE. THUS, WHEN HE IS GETTING HIGH, HE WATCHES HOW EVERYONE ACTS AROUND HIM AND HE IS ELIMINATING THOSE WHO HE

DOES NOT WANT TO COME BACK TO HIS HOUSE. YOU WILL NOT SEE HIM STANDING ON STREET CORNERS LIKE A CRACKHEAD. HE HAS HIS DRUGS COMING TO HIM AND HE HUSTLES HIS HITS AT HIS HOUSE. WOE! DRUG DEALERS FLOCK TO HIS HOUSE LIKE WOMEN ON DRUGS AND HE CHARGES THEM TO THE GAME FOR ANOTHER PIECE OF DOPE. HE THINK IT IS AN INSULT FOR HIM TO BE CALLED A CRACKHEAD. HIS KNOWLEDGE OF THE GAME KEEPS DRUG DEALERS PAYING HIM. HE KNOWS HOW TO CAKE IT, SHAKE IT, AND BAKE IT. UNLIKE A CRACKHEAD, HE WILL NOT PUT HIS LIFE ON THE LINE TRYING TO SELL A DRUG DEALER'S DOPE. BESIDES, THEY NEED TO USE HIS PLACE TO COOK IT AND HE STEALS HIS HITS OUT THE JAR. A CRACK SMOKER KNOWS IT IS BAD ENOUGH THAT HE USES DRUGS, LET ALONE TRYING TO SELL IT. HIS KNOWLEDGE OF HIS ADDICTION KEEPS HIM ALIVE IN THE STREETS, BUT TO A CRACKHEAD, BEATING A DOPE DEALER FOR DRUGS, IS LIKE A DRUG DEALER BEATING HIM FOR HIS MONEY. IT IS ALL A PART OF THE DOPE GAME AND IN HAVING NO RESPECT FOR THE GAME, IT EVENTUALLY COSTS THEM THEIR LIVES.

CRACK SMOKER IN HIS CLEVERNESS

A CRACK SMOKER IN HIS CLEVERNESS CAN USE DRUGS OFF AND ON UP TO 40 YEARS AND REMAIN ALIVE, BUT IF GOD HAS NOT DELIVERED YOU FROM DRUGS, YOU WILL ALWAYS BE A DRUG USER. UNLESS GOD DELIVERS YOU FROM DRUGS, YOU WILL ALWAYS BE ADDICTED TO DRUGS, AND UNLESS GOD DELIVERS YOU FROM DRUGS YOU WILL DIE USING DRUGS. YOU CAN BE DETAINED SIX YEARS IN PRISON, STAY LOCKED IN YOUR HOUSE FOR SIX MONTHS, OR GO TO REHAB SIX HOURS EACH DAY AND YOU WILL STILL USE DRUGS. UNLESS GOD DELIVERS YOU FROM DRUGS, YOU WILL SEE A PIECE OF DOPE AND WANT IT BECAUSE YOU HAVE NOT BEEN DELIVERED BY GOD FROM THE DEMONS OF YOUR ADDICTION. YOU JUST UP AND QUIT AND THAT IS NOT GOOD ENOUGH WHEN YOU ARE DEALING WITH THE DEVIL. MANY LIVES HAVE BEEN LOST BY THOSE WHO JUST UP AND QUIT. THEY WERE NOT DELIVERED BY GOD. THEY

WERE DECEIVED BY SATAN TO TAKE A BIG HIT AND HE TORTURED THEIR LITTLE, FRIGHTENED SOUL TO DEATH. MY LORD! STAYING AWAY FROM DRUGS DOES NOT KEEP YOU FROM BEING ADDICTED TO DRUGS, NOR WILL IT KEEP DRUGS AWAY FROM YOU. YOU MUST SEEK GOD WITH ALL YOUR MIND, BODY, AND SOUL (Luke 10:27) AND GOD WILL DELIVER YOU FROM THE DEMONS OF YOUR ADDICTION.

GOD'S DELIVERANCE FROM DEMONS

THERE IS A DIFFERENCE IN BEING DELIVERED FROM DRUGS BY GOD AND STAYING ADDICTED TO DRUG BY THE DEVIL. YOU CAN STOP USING DRUGS RIGHT NOW ON YOUR OWN, BUT THE DEVIL WILL STILL HAVE YOU ADDICTED. YOU HAVE NOT BEEN DELIVERED BY GOD FROM THE DEMONS OF YOUR ADDICTION. WHEN GOD DELIVERS YOU FROM DRUGS, YOU WILL NOT USE DRUGS BECAUSE GOD WILL CAST THE DEMONIC SPIRITS OUT OF THE ADDICTION. THE TASTE FOR DRUGS WILL NO LONGER BE IN YOUR MOUTH AND THE CRAVING FOR DRUGS WILL NO LONGER BE IN YOUR MIND. GOD WILL DELIVER YOU FROM THE DEMONS THAT ARE IN THE ADDICTION. IT IS THE DEMON IN THE ADDICTION THAT KEEPS YOU ADDICTED. YOU ARE ADDICTED TO WATER, FOOD, AND THE VERY THINGS YOU DO HABITUALLY ON A DAILY BASIS YET, THERE ARE NO DEMONS IN THESE ADDICTIVE THINGS. THEREFORE, GOD WILL NOT TAKE THESE ADDICTIONS FROM YOU NOR WILL YOU DIE FROM THESE ADDICTIONS.

SOME ADDICTIONS DEMONIC

FOR SOME, ADDICTIONS ARE DEMONIC AND YOUR DRUG ADDICTION HAS A DEMON IN IT. YOU NEED GOD TO TAKE THE DEMONS OUT OF THAT ADDICTION SO THAT THERE WILL BE NO ADDICTION. WHEN GOD DELIVERS YOU FROM THE DEMONS OF AN ADDICTION, THE DEMONS ARE NO LONGER ATTACHED TO THAT ADDICTION. FOR WHATSOEVER BE YOUR DRUG AS

AN ADDICTION, ONLY GOD CAN SEPARATE YOU FROM THE DEMONS THAT ARE IN THE ADDICTION. WHO ELSE, OTHER THAN GOD, CAN BRING BACK A DAY THAT HAS ALREADY PASSED? WHO ELSE, OTHER THAN GOD, CAN WEIGH OUT A POUND OF FIRE, AND WHO ELSE OTHER THAN GOD CAN CAST THE DEMONS OUT OF YOUR ADDICTION WHILE DRUGS ARE STILL IN YOUR MOUTH AND THE DEVIL'S LIE IS RUNNING THROUGH YOUR VEINS? YOU MUST TRUST IN THE LORD WITH ALL YOUR MIND, BODY, AND SOUL AND GOD WILL DELIVER FROM THE DEMONS OF YOUR ADDICTION. HOWEVER LONG IT WILL TAKE FOR YOU TO FIND THE GOD IN YOU, WOULD BE THE SAME LENGTH OF TIME IT WILL TAKE GOD TO DELIVER YOU. YOUR DELIVERANCE FROM AN ADDICTION COMES FROM YOU DOING THE RIGHT THING YOU HARD-HEADED, BLACK SHEEP! GOD IS WAITING ON YOU TO DO THE RIGHT THING. HE WILL DELIVER YOU WHEN YOU START DOING THE RIGHT THINGS. WHEN YOU FIND THE LORD, THERE IS NOT A DEVIL IN HELL THAT CAN STOP GOD FROM DELIVERING YOU. THERE IS NOT ONE DEVIL IN HELL EXCEPT YOU AND GOD IS WAITING ON YOU RIGHT NOW TO MAKE THE RIGHT CHOICE. ALL YOU HAVE TO DO IS THE RIGHT THING AND THAT IS TO ACCEPT THE LORD, SO GOD CAN DELIVER YOU FROM THE DEMONS OF YOUR ADDICTION. GOD WILL NOT DELIVER YOU FROM A DRUG ADDICTION BY DOING UNGODLY THINGS.

YOU MUST BECOME GODLY

HOW DO YOU STOP USING DRUGS? YOU MUST BECOME MORE GODLY IN YOUR ADDICTION AND IT IS JUST THAT SIMPLE! UNDERSTAND YOU! BY YOU BEING A CLEVER CRACK SMOKER AS YOU SAY YOU ARE, RATHER THAN A FUMBLING CRACKHEAD AS YOU SAY YOU ARE NOT, YOU MIGHT BE ABLE TO HIDE YOUR ADDICTION FROM OTHERS, BUT YOU ARE NOT FOOLING ANYONE, BUT YOU. YOU ARE STILL ADDICTED TO DRUGS AND YOU HAVE NOT BEEN DELIVERED BY GOD FROM THE DEMONS OF YOUR ADDICTION. OVER THE YEARS YOU MAY HAVE LEARNED HOW TO RATION YOUR HITS, BUT YOU HAVEN'T

BEEN DELIVERED BY GOD FROM THE DEMONS OF YOUR ADDICTION. KNOWING HOW TO MANIPULATE DRUGS DOES NOT KEEP PILLS OUT OF YOUR MOUTH, SMOKE OUT OF YOUR HEAD, OR THE NEDDLE OUT YOUR VEINS. YOU MIGHT CONSIDER YOURSELF A CRACK SMOKER RATHER THAN A CRACK HEAD, BUT WHAT DIFFERENCE DOES IT MAKE? YOU BOTH USE DRUGS! YOU ARE STILL ADDICTED AND YOU HAVE NOT BEEN DELIVERED BY GOD FROM THE DEMONS OF YOUR ADDICTION! OF COURSE, YOU WILL KNOW DRUG ADDICTS WHO WILL LET YOU USE THEIR PIPES, BUT IF THEY DO, YOU BETTER NOT PUSH IT. WOE! YOU HAVE TO BE A USER TO KNOW THESE WORDS. IF NOT, WHY ARE YOU READING THIS BOOK? YOU ARE EITHER THINKING ABOUT USING DRUGS, HAVE USED DRUGS, OR SOMEONE YOU CARE ABOUT IS ON DRUGS.

THE SAME YOU

WHAT? THIS IS YOU? AND YOU ARE NOT TRYING TO STOP USING DRUGS?! YOU DO NOT WANT TO KNOW HOW TO STOP USING DRUGS? YOU JUST WANT KNOWLEDGE OF YOUR ADDICTION? YOU WANT SOMEONE TO BECOME YOUR ENABLER?! YOU WANT SOMEONE TO MONITOR YOUR USAGE AND WAKE YOU UP WHEN IT IS TIME TO TAKE ANOTHER HIT. THAT WAY YOU CAN USE DRUGS UNTIL THE DAY YOU DIE AND MAYBE, JUST MAYBE, THE FAMILY WILL LEAVE YOU AND YOUR DRUG ADDICTION ALONE! SO THAT YOU COULD JUST SMOKE YOUR MISERABLE LIFE AWAY AND ENJOY YOUR OWN DEATH. WOE! THE MAN IS TRAPPED. THE DEMONS HAVE TRAPPED THE MAN IN THEIR ADDICTIONS BECAUSE HE FELL IN LOVE WITH DRUGS. TODAY HE IS CONVINCED HE IS A DRUG ADDICT, AND IN HIS THREE-DIMENSIONAL DECEPTIONS, HE HAS BEEN DEMONIZED, DYING, AND IS NEAR DEATH. WOE! HE WALKS AROUND DAILY IN HIS SEARCH FOR DRUGS AND HE WILL NOT STOP UNTIL HE RUNS OUT OF HITS OR WAYS OF GETTING MORE DRUGS. WOE!

BLACK SHEEP, THE LORD HAS SPOKEN ON ADDICTION AS DEMONIC AND YOU CAN NOT CONTROL EVIL. THUS, HOW CAN YOU CONTROL SOMETHING THAT YOU DID NOT CREATE? GOD CREATED EVIL AND YOUR DRUG ADDICTION HAS COME UPON YOU FOR NOT SERVING GOD. YOU KNOW THE TRUTH, BUT YET YOU EXPECT GOD TO DELIVER YOU FROM WHAT YOU WANT TO DO? YOU MUST SERVE HIM! "YOU ARE NOT YOUR OWN" (Romans 8:9) THEREFORE, SURRENDER UNTO GOD THAT WHICH IS GOD AND THAT WHICH BE NOTHING MORE THAN ONE'S SELF, MADE UNTO THE GLORY OF GOD (Isaiah 43:7). YOU ARE GOD'S CREATION, (Colossians 1:16) BUT SO IS EVIL. GOD DID NOT CREATE YOU TO BE AS EVIL, BUT TO KNOW EVIL, THAT YOU MAY BE GOOD (2 Timothy 3:13).

YOU'RE THE BLACK SHEEP

YET, YOU ARE THE BLACK SHEEP AND AGAIN YOU HAVE REFUSED GOD'S INSTRUCTIONS. YOU HAVE REFUSED TO BE GOOD AND SEEK THE LORD TO DELIVER YOU. YOU HAVE CHOSEN EVIL AND YOUR ADDICTION HAS BECOME YOU. YOU WERE BORN HOLY, BUT YOUR ADDICTION HAS MADE YOU UNHOLY. YOUR ADDICTION IS BEYOND YOU, BUT NOT GOD, AND IT IS GOD WHO DELIVERS YOU, NOT YOU! YOU WERE BOUGHT AND PAID FOR WITH THE BLOOD OF JESUS CHRIST. THEREFORE, THE BLOOD OF THE LORD BE UPON YOU AND YOU NO LONGER BELONG TO YOU. YOU MUST GIVE UNTO THE LORD YOUR MIND, BODY, AND SOUL TO BE DELIVERED FROM YOUR ADDICTION (Romans 4:1-25). OTHERWISE, GOD WILL NOT DELIVER YOU FROM THE EVIL THAT WILL DESTROY YOU. THE LORD HAS SPOKEN ON ADDICTION AS DEMONIC. YET, ONLY JESUS CHRIST CAN DELIVER YOU FROM YOUR SINS. "WHILE IT IS SAID, TODAY IF YE WILL HEAR HIS VOICE, HARDEN NOT YOUR HEARTS, AS IN THE DAY OF PROVOCATION" (Hebrew 3:15). THUS, UNDERSTAND YOU! TO FORSAKE GOD'S WORD IS DEATH, BUT TO ACCEPT GOD'S INSTRUCTION IS TO ENJOY LONGEVITY OF LIFE.

YOU HAVE REFUSED GOD'S INSTRUCTIONS

YOU ARE THE BLACK SHEEP WHO, AS OF YET, HAS REFUSED GOD'S INSTRUCTIONS (Proverbs 1: 1-33). YOU HAVE NOT SOUGHT THE LORD AS GOD HAS ADMONISHED YOU. THEREFORE, THE DEMONS OF YOUR ADDICTION ARE GOING TO DESTROY YOU! MY LORD, THEIR EVIL WILL BECOME YOU, AND YOU WILL DO ANYTHING FOR DRUGS. YOU WILL DO WHATEVER THESE DEMONS WOULD HAVE YOU TO DO, FOR THESE ARE THE THINGS IN YOUR ADDICTION THAT YOU WILL DO BECAUSE THE DRUGS WILL BECOME YOU. THUS, AS OF YET, AGAIN, I ADMONISH YOU BLACK SHEEP, DO NOT YOU SMOKE YOUR BURIAL EXPENSES TO DISPOSE OF YOUR OWN ROTTEN CARCASS! NOT ONLY HAVE YOU BEEN A BURDEN TO THE FAMILY WHILE YOU HAVE LIVED, BUT YOU WOULD BE AN EVEN A GREATER BURDEN AFTER YOUR DEATH. WOE! ARE YOU SURE YOU ARE A BLACK SHEEP, A WOLF IN SHEEPS CLOTHING, OR A GOAT? THEN UNDERSTAND YOU! HOW DO YOU STOP USING DRUGS? DO EXACTLY WHAT THE LORD SAYS DO AND GOD WILL DELIVER YOU, FOR IN YOUR ADDICTION YOUR FAMILY DEPENDS ON YOU TO DO THE RIGHT THING, BUT WHAT CAN THEY EVER EXPECT FROM YOU EXCEPT YOUR WORST?! WOE!